A Brave New Series

GLOBAL ISSUES
IN A CHANGING WORLD

This new series of short, accessible think pieces deals with leading global issues of relevance to humanity today. Intended for the enquiring reader and social activists in the North and the South, as well as students, the books explain what is at stake and question conventional ideas and policies. Drawn from many different parts of the world, the series' authors pay particular attention to the needs and interests of ordinary people, whether living in the rich industrial or the developing countries. They all share a common objective: to help stimulate new thinking and social action in the opening years of the new century.

Global Issues in a Changing World is a joint initiative by Zed Books in collaboration with a number of partner publishers and non-governmental organizations around the world. By working together, we intend to maximize the relevance and availability of the books published in the series.

PARTICIPATING NGOs

Both ENDS, Amsterdam
Catholic Institute of International Relations, London
Corner House, Sturminster Newton
Council on International and Public Affairs, New York
Dag Hammarskjöld Foundation, Uppsala
Development GAP, Washington DC
Focus on the Global South, Bangkok
Inter Pares, Ot
Public Interest Research
Third World Netwo
Third World Network
World Development Mo

GW00566517

About this Series

'Communities in the South are facing great difficulties in coping with global trends. I hope this brave new series will throw much-needed light on the issues ahead and help us choose the right options.'
Martin Khor, Director, Third World Network

'There is no more important campaign than our struggle to bring the global economy under democratic control. But the issues are fearsomely complex. This Global Issues series is a valuable resource for the committed campaigner and the educated citizen.'
Barry Coates, Director, World Development Movement (WDM)

'Zed Books has long provided an inspiring list about the issues that touch and change people's lives. The Global Issues series is another dimension of Zed's fine record, allowing access to a range of subjects and authors that, to my knowledge, very few publishers have tried. I strongly recommend these new, powerful titles and this exciting series.'
John Pilger, author

'We are all part of a generation that actually has the means to eliminate extreme poverty world-wide. Our task is to harness the forces of globalisation for the benefit of working people, their families and their communities – that is our collective duty. The Global Issues series makes a powerful contribution to the global campaign for justice, sustainable and equitable development, and peaceful progress.'
Glenys Kinnock, MEP

A GLOBAL ISSUES TITLE

ISLAM & JIHAD

Prejudice versus Reality

A.G. Noorani

Zed Books
London and New York

University Press Ltd
Dhaka

White Lotus Co. Ltd
Bangkok

Fernwood
Nova Scotia

David Philip
Cape Town

Islam and Jihad
was first published in 2002 by

In Bangladesh: The University Press Ltd, Red Crescent Building,
114 Motijheel C/A, PO Box 2611, Dhaka 1000

In Burma, Cambodia, Laos, Thailand and Vietnam:
White Lotus Co. Ltd, GPO Box 1141, Bangkok 10501, Thailand

In Canada: Fernwood, 8422 St Margaret's Bay Road (Hwy 3),
Site 2A, Box 5, Black Point, Nova Scotia B0J 1B0

In Southern Africa: David Philip (an imprint of New Africa Books),
99 Garfield Road, Claremont 7700, South Africa

In the rest of the world:
Zed Books Ltd, 7 Cynthia Street, London N1 9JF, UK and
Room 400, 175 Fifth Avenue, New York, NY 10010, USA

www.zedbooks.demon.co.uk

Distributed in the USA exclusively by Palgrave, a division of
St Martin's Press, LLC, 175 Fifth Avenue, New York, NY 10010

Copyright © A.G. Noorani 2002
Cover design by Andrew Corbett
Set in 10/13 pt Monotype Bembo by Long House, Cumbria, UK
Printed and bound in the United Kingdom by Cox & Wyman, Reading

The rights of the author of this work have been asserted by him
in accordance with the Copyright, Designs and Patents Act, 1988.
All rights reserved.

A catalogue record for this book is available from the British Library
US CIP data is available from the Library of Congress
Canadian CIP data is available from the National Library of Canada

ISBN 1 55266 098 2 Pb (Canada)
ISBN 0 86486 602 X Pb (Southern Africa)
ISBN 1 84277 270 8 Hb (Zed Books)
ISBN 1 84277 271 6 Pb (Zed Books)

CONTENTS

To the memory of
SYED AHMAD KHAN
(1817–1898)

Founder of Aligarh Muslim University

A great teacher and reformer, devout Muslim
and committed rationalist

ABOUT THE AUTHOR

A.G. NOORANI is a lawyer and political commentator. His columns appear in *The Hindustan Times*, *Frontline*, *Economic and Political Weekly* and *Dainik Bhaskar*. He is the author of *The Kashmir Question*, *Badruddin Tyabji*, *Ministers' Misconduct*, *Brezhnev's Plan for Asian Security*, *The Presidential System*, *The Trial of Bhagat Singh* and *Constitutional Questions in India*. His most recent book is *The RSS and the BJP: A Division of Labour* (LeftWord 2000). He is currently working on another book, *The Kashmir Question Revisited*.

PREFACE

This book would not have been written but for a strong suggestion last October by my brother Mushtaq, who lives in Bangalore. He was disturbed at the reaction to the attacks on the World Trade Centre on September 11, 2001 in the United States, in India, and elsewhere in many parts of the world. There were strange comments in certain sections among both non-Muslims and Muslims. Mushtaq had in mind a book for the lay reader, written in simple prose, to correct misimpressions about Islam in the minds of non-Muslims as well as Muslims; not an apologia, but a corrective.

Neither he nor friends who assisted me are responsible in any manner for the book as it has finally emerged. The responsibility for factual errors or flaws in analysis is mine exclusively. Once started, the book wrote itself, as it were. I have expressed in it thoughts I have long wanted to express, on Western misperceptions and misrepresentation of Islam, as well as on the Muslims' refusal to reflect on the fundamentals of Islam and on the abiding relevance of the religion to our times. The so-called Islamic fundamentalist is an imposter. He has misused a noble faith as a political weapon. Of course Islam does have a political vision; but it is far removed from the Islam which very many Muslims and most non-Muslims imagine it to be.

The challenge to intellectual creativity is particularly important in this region. In South Asia live one-third of the world's 1.3 billion Muslims. Western Europe has six million Muslims; the

United States has three million of whom 10,000 serve in its armed forces.

The fundamentalists' cries of jihad and the Islamic state have no validity in the religion and bear no relevance to the times. Islam does; and ever will.

I am indebted to my friend Mr Muhammad Hamid Ansari, Vice-Chancellor of Aligarh Muslim University and a distinguished former diplomat, for tracing in the AMU's library a copy of Maulvi Chiragh Ali's nineteenth century classic on jihad. The original was in a frail condition. A dedicated bibliophile, Mr Muhammad Ahmed, launched the Idarah-I-Adabiayat in Delhi to reprint such works. Fortunately, AMU's library had this reprint as well. Frédéric Grare, Director, Centre de Sciences Humaines, in New Delhi, was kind enough to read the manuscript and make useful suggestions. Last but not least, publication of the book would not have been possible without the interest shown and the considerable industry expended by my friend Sudhanva Deshpande and his colleagues at LeftWord Books, New Delhi, the first publishers of this book. For the subsequent editions, thanks are due to my friend Ms Ameena Saiyid, Managing Editor, Oxford University Press, Karachi, for her encouragement and enthusiasm, and to Mr Robert Molteno, Editor, Zed Books, London, for his keen interest in this work. None of the above, of course, are responsible for what I have written.

If the book prods keener interest in the subject, and further study and reflection, I shall be content.

A word about the text: in my writing, I have dispensed with italicization and capitalization of Islamic terms. In quotes, however, I have kept the original spellings, capitalization, and italicization. Wherever words in quotes have been italicized for stress, that is my addition.

A.G. NOORANI • *Mumbai* • *June 2002*

CHAPTER 1

INTRODUCTION
'THE SPECTRE
OF ISLAM'

'*A spectre is haunting Europe – the spectre of Communism. All the Powers of old Europe have entered into a holy alliance to exorcise this spectre; Pope and Czar, Metternich and Guizot, French Radicals and German police-spies.*

'*Where is the party in opposition that has not been decried as communistic by its opponents in power? Where the opposition that has not hurled back the branding reproach of Communism, against the more advanced opposition parties, as well as against its reactionary adversaries?*

'*Two things result from this fact:*

'*I. Communism is already acknowledged by all European Powers to be itself a Power.*

'*II. It is high time that Communists should openly, in the face of the whole world, publish their views, their aims, their tendencies, and meet this nursery tale of the Spectre of Communism with a Manifesto of the party itself.*'

If adapted to the situation we face today, and have witnessed in the last two decades and more, these opening lines of the *Manifesto of the Communist Party*, which Karl Marx and Friedrich Engels wrote in 1848, will yield a startlingly similar result. 'A spectre of Islam' haunts the West, and a monolithic and violent Islam is demonized as a 'threat to Western civilization' and to the West's unchallenged power across the continents.

The spectre of Islam

As far back as February 2, 1995, the *International Herald Tribune* reported from Paris that NATO had decided 'to open talks with five North African and Middle Eastern States to develop a joint strategy to combat the security threat posed by Islamic fundamentalism'. They made an odd bunch, these shining examples of democracy – Egypt, Israel, Morocco, Tunisia and Mauritania. *The Washington Post's* Paris correspondent, William Drozdiak, reported also that NATO's Secretary-General, Willy Claes, had told a security conference, held in Germany a few days earlier, that in the five years since the collapse of communism in Eastern Europe, Islamic militancy had emerged as perhaps the single gravest threat to the alliance and Western security. Algeria was omitted from the list of NATO's prospective partners because the alliance did not want to be seen as 'overtly taking sides' with the army in its battle to suppress the Islamic Salvation Front and other armed Muslim groups.

The West had no problems with Saddam Hussein's attack on Iran in 1980. Iraq's invasion of Kuwait, a decade later, made all the difference. Shortly after the Gulf War broke out, Strobe Talbott wrote an article in *Time*[1] entitled 'Living with Saddam'. His fears covered a vast part of the globe: 'No matter how and when the war ends, Islamic rage already threatens the stability of traditionally pro-Western regimes from Morocco to Jordan to Pakistan'. He served as Deputy Secretary of State in the Clinton administration not long after.

To be sure, there were some who disagreed with this view. Patrick J. Buchanan, for instance, had written: 'To some Americans, searching for a new enemy against whom to test our mettle and power, after the death of Communism, Islam is the preferred antagonist. But to declare Islam an enemy of the United States is to declare a Second Cold War that is unlikely to end in the same resounding victory as the first'.[2] In 1992 appeared the first edition of Prof. John L. Esposito's excellent book, *The Islamic Threat*,[3] which debunked many myths.

The 'nursery tales', however, were spread with yet greater

ardour. In July 1993, *Foreign Affairs* published Samuel P. Huntington's seminal article, 'The Clash of Civilizations'. His thesis appeared in expanded book form three years later.[4] For Huntington, the principal clash was, of course, between the West and Islam. He wrote: 'The underlying problem for the West is not Islamic fundamentalism. It is Islam, a different civilization whose people are convinced of the superiority of their culture and are obsessed with the inferiority of their power. The problem for Islam is not the CIA or the US Department of Defence. It is the West, a different civilization whose people are convinced of the universality of their culture and believe that their superior, if declining, power imposes on them the obligation to extend that culture throughout the world. These are the basic ingredients that fuel conflict between Islam and the West'.[5]

Spurious theories thrive on sweeping assertions and misrepresentations. Where is the conflict between the Islamic Saudi Arabia and 'the West', to go no further? A few pages before the above quote, Huntington quotes Esposito as saying that the 'historical dynamics of Christian–Muslim relations often found the two communities in competition and locked at times in deadly combat for power, land and souls'.[6] If one traces this passage back to Esposito's book,[7] it becomes clear that he was describing a *past*, albeit one whose memories linger still, because of the West's politics. But Esposito's views on the *present*, and his hopes and expectations for the future, clash with Huntington's dire prophecies: 'Talk of a political and cultural conflict could be seen not only in fears of confrontation but also in assertions that Islam is incompatible with democracy and modernity. The charge that political Islam is inherently militant became an excuse for suppressing movements and closing the door to democratization in many Muslim countries. These beliefs and attitudes affected the policies of governments and the actions of Islamic activists in the Muslim world and in the West. At the dawn of the twenty-first century, placing global events and fears within a balanced context has never been more important'.[8]

Muslim bigotry and mindless violence

But the 'nursery tales' peddled in books such as *The Rage of Islam*, *The Global Intifada*, *The Roots of Muslim Rage*, *The Dagger of Islam*, *The Holy Killers of Islam* and the TV film *The Sword of Islam* had done their work. Prejudice against Islam has existed even at the best of times. Now, a whole clime of adversarial relationship was created. This, in turn, was strengthened by expressions of bigotry and senseless acts of violence in some Muslim countries; for example, the assassination of the Egyptian President Anwar Sadat in October 1981 by members of al-Jihad. The attack was led by Lt. Khalid al-Islambouli. The movement's ideologue was Abdal Salam Faraj. The man who issued the fatwa authorizing the assassination was the blind preacher Sheikh Umar Abdal Rahman. The al-Jihad movement condemned as traitors the older Muslim Brotherhood, founded by Hasan al-Banna in 1928. Its ideologue, Sayyid Qutb, was sent to the gallows by President Gamal Abdel Nasser in 1966. Sayyid Qutb was much influenced by the writings of Maulana Abul A'la Maududi.

Sadat's assassination was preceded by the Islamic Revolution in Iran in 1979 and was followed by a series of gruesome acts of violence in the next two decades. In 1997, 58 foreign tourists were killed in Luxor, Egypt, in a bid to cripple the country's economy.

Algeria presents a special case. There were massacres in Algeria by both the army and the militants. The Islamic Salvation Front (FIS) drew its inspiration from the Quran but its main achievement was as 'a social movement able to articulate the discontent among the rapidly growing section of the population that was bearing the brunt of the worsening economic hardship'.[9] The

FIS won 47 per cent of the vote and 188 of the 231 seats in the first ballot of elections to the national legislature in which no second ballot was required. The ruling FLN won only 15 seats. A second ballot was due for the remaining seats in which no candidate had achieved 50 per cent of the vote. It was never held. On January 12, 1992, tanks rolled out on to the streets of Algiers. The FIS was banned for attempted 'insurrection against the State'. Algeria has known no peace in the decade since.

The crackdown had predictable results. If the army was afraid that, once in power, the FIS would not hold free elections thereafter, militant sections of the FIS were afraid they would have to compromise with other groups. 'By 1993, the Islamist organizations that had retained a commitment to the democratic process curtailed by the military coup saw their influence increasingly overshadowed by the appearance of a new organization that from the outset rejected the democratic path followed by the FIS and sought power purely through armed struggle. This was the Jamaat Islamiyya Mousalaha, the Armed Islamic Group or GIA.'[10] There was not a murmur of protest by the West at the murder of democracy in 1992.

The army coup sent a dangerous message to extremists elsewhere. In the 1990s, the US military was attacked in Riyadh (1995) and Dhahran (1996) in Saudi Arabia. On August 7, 1998, American embassies in Tanzania and Kenya were bombed, killing 263 people and injuring more than 5,000. In retaliation, the US attacked sites in Sudan and Afghanistan on August 27, which it alleged were used for training terrorists.

Fears of global 'Islamic Terror', kindled by the bombing of the World Trade Centre in New York in March 1993, received support from the incidents that followed. By this time Osama bin Laden emerged as the leader of the 'Arab Afghans' – Arabs who had joined the 'jihad' in Afghanistan against the Soviet forces, under the auspices of the United States' CIA, Pakistan's ISI and

Saudi Arabia's intelligence under the leadership of Prince Turki
bin Faisal al-Saud (who was sacked from his post on 1 September
2001). Scion of a prominent and rich Saudi family, bin Laden
developed a strong antipathy towards the US on his return to
Saudi Arabia in 1991, on two grounds – the Gulf War and, more
so, the continued presence of American forces on the soil of his
country.

Censures on the ruling family, the House of Saud, cost him
his citizenship. He moved to Sudan in 1994 and became a militant
activist, avowedly in the cause of Islam. As we shall see, there was
not a spark of originality or even coherence in the ideas he put
forth; that is, if his fulminations can at all be dignified as 'ideas'.
American charges that he used Sudan as a base for terrorist activity
prompted its government to demand his departure from its
territory. He returned to Afghanistan, which the Taliban had by
then almost completely taken over. He, in turn, took over the
Taliban regime in all but name. The US suspected him of funding
terrorist groups and of complicity in the bombing of the World
Trade Centre in 1993, the bombings in Riyadh and Dhahran, the
killings in Luxor, and the bombing of the American embassies in
Tanzania and Kenya.

As far back as 1985, 'bin Laden had collected enough millions
from his family and construction company wealth and from
donations from wealthy Arab Gulf merchant families, to organize
al-Qaida, the Islamic Salvation Foundation, to support the jihad.
He established a network of al-Qaida recruitment centres in Saudi
Arabia, Egypt and Pakistan, through which he recruited, enlisted
and sheltered thousands of Arab volunteers', John K. Cooley,
correspondent for ABC News, recorded.[11] Not long ago, 'he
seemed to both Saudi intelligence and the CIA an ideal choice for
the leading role he began to play' in Afghanistan.[12]

'Whose Islam are we performing?'

It was against this background that the attacks on the World Trade Centre and the Pentagon took place on September 11, 2001. In sheer malevolence, brutality, and scale they outstripped the previous attacks. American resentment and anger at what was nothing short of an act of war are as understandable as the calm and discipline which the people showed are admirable. But in the aftermath, the effects of the clime fostered in recent decades began to be felt by Asian Americans, especially by Arab Americans and Muslim Americans.

All the pent up prejudices and emotions came to the fore. American Asians were asked questions about their loyalty and began to ask themselves searching questions about their own identity years after they had adopted the United States of America as their country. One anguished but highly intelligent cry from an Asian American of Pakistani origin articulated the emotions they felt, and bears quotation *in extenso*. This is from Dr Fawzia Afzal Khan, who is Professor of English at the Montclair State University in New Jersey. Her predicament reflects questions of identity that face minorities in times of crisis like the attack on the WTC: 'Here I was, a 43 years old Pakistani-American-Muslim-Feminist-English-Professor-Singer-Actor-Scholar-Critic-Wife-Mother, being asked to take sides, to reduce the complexities and contradictions of my multiple identities to one or the other label: Muslim or Secular, Islamist or Feminist, Pakistani or American and the greatest of them all – "pro-terrorist" or "pro-civilization". Sadly and unambiguously, I have been forced to realize that the peculiar identity that I and many others wanted to cling to, of a community more "mine" than others, a "Pakistani-American" community, and a larger pan-Islamic one, is nothing but a mirage – a tenuous identity at best, a falsehood at worst. Why?

'I think the answer resides, at least partially, in the problem with identity labels in general. These labels conceal more than they reveal, for in the attempt to unify people holding diverse and often mutually contradictory points of view into one whole as defined by nation, religion, sexuality, ethnicity, gender, race and so on, such labels suppress the heterogeneity of dissenting, questioning voices; the voices of people like myself, who are both "inside" and "outside".

'I feel angry and alienated when my seven-year-old son tells me that a neighbour has asked him, "Are you American or what? How come you don't fly the American flag outside your house?" Is flying the flag the only way now to live out my American-ness? When I visit my Egyptian-American friends and see a huge American flag covering the entire front of their house, I feel depressed. When I visit Pakistani-American friends for a dinner party a week after September 11 and they tell me to fly the flag, as they all are "in gratitude for what this country has given us", I feel angry and alienated and somehow, ashamed for them. . . .

'Why am I now a spokesperson for Islam? Playing a role not of my choice, I am forced to realize that the parts available to me either "inside" or "outside" the proverbial whale, whether the whale be America or the Islamic world, are as limited and limiting as the stages available to perform them on. The leading male actors on the stage of the Western Alliance are telling me I must choose either to play a heroine of civilization or a scarf-toting terrorist.'

She asked herself, 'Whose Islam are we performing, I want to scream. Does anyone care? *And what, ultimately, does the present crisis have to do with Islam? Which Islamic text is being performed for which audience, where?*'

The resentment was perfectly justified. She quotes a colleague she respected, who wrote, 'This attack on America is an attack by Islamists who hate the values of tolerance and democracy and liberal secularism that this country stands for'. 'This opinion', she says, 'was echoed by a chorus. When I find myself issuing a rejoinder pointing out that there are many varieties of "Islamists" out there, that the term is hardly reducible to the fanatical extremism of the Taliban, I once again feel angered and alienated because I have been reduced to "taking sides" in what is in the final analysis, a set-up, a completely bogus, morally bankrupt, utterly disingenuous choice.'[13]

Indian Muslims are not unfamiliar with such school boy questions. In the UK Norman Tebbitt posed them to the Asian community.

As in the McCarthy era, there were significant protests and significant silences on the violations of civil liberties of Asians and Arabs (Muslims being singled out in both categories). The US Justice Department's plan to question 5,000 students from Muslim countries was rightly criticized as 'racial profiling'. To their credit, some local authorities refused to cooperate. However, *The Economist's* Washington D.C. correspondent enthusiastically approved of the official measures: 'But all the hijackers and their presumed accomplices were young Muslim males. Questioning old Chinese ladies, just for "balance" seems pretty pointless'.[14] Over a thousand persons were detained.

Flora Lewis, in contrast, was more forthcoming: 'Both the White House and the Attorney General have argued that terrorists do not deserve constitutional protection of the rule of law, that military tribunals or whatever the President considers necessary for their punishment are themselves a guarantee of the liberties they would attack'.[15]

Although London-based, pages of the stridently pro-American weekly *The Economist* provide a good flavour of the atmosphere in the United States and in the West at large. It is, remember, a serious journal, though some of its headlines would make one think it is a tabloid. On September 15, in the first issue after September 11, it asked the question 'Who is to blame?' and confidently delivered this answer: 'Much of the evidence points towards *Islamic* extremists *in general* and Osama bin Laden in particular'.[16] This model of precision referred to a detailed report which said: 'Investigators have already turned up evidence pointing to *Arab* involvement'. A few lines later, it warned: 'But even if, as seems likely, the authorities soon establish that the perpetrators were *Muslim* extremists, they will find it harder to work out who sent them'. We would do well to remember that the leader of the Marxist militant Popular Front for the Liberation of Palestine was Georges Habash, a Christian. In the same issue a report from Lahore injected a dose of realism: 'In its understandable rage for justice, America may be tempted to overlook one uncomfortable fact. Its own policies in Afghanistan a decade and more ago helped to create both Osama bin Laden and the fundamentalist Taliban regime that shelters him.

'*The notion of jihad, or holy war, had almost ceased to exist in the Muslim world after the tenth century until it was revived, with American encouragement, to fire an international pan-Islamic movement after the Soviet invasion of Afghanistan in 1979.* For the next ten years, the CIA and Saudi intelligence together pumped in billions of dollars' worth of arms and ammunition through Pakistan's Inter-Services Intelligence agency (ISI) to the many mujahideen groups fighting in Afghanistan. . . . For the past ten years that deadly brew has spread its ill-effects widely. Pakistan has suffered terrible destabilization. But the Afghanis, the name given to the young Muslim men who fought the infidel in Afghanistan, have carried their jihad far beyond: to the corrupt kingdoms of the Gulf, to the repressive states of the southern Mediterranean, and now, perhaps, to New York and Washington DC.'[17]

How 'Islamic' was 9/11?

Who *was* it, then, militant Arab nationalists, or militant Islamists?

The former wreak vengeance for wrongs done by Western colonialism and the corrupt rulers it props up. The latter strive to
establish an Islamic State. Only a political illiterate would confuse
the two.

The Economist returned to the charge in its next issue dated
September 22, 2001: 'Who is to blame? The simple answer – the
suicide attackers, and those behind them – is hardly adequate'. It
cited, refreshingly, instances of the US's 'arrogant, even hypo-
critical' policies, only to return to its defence.[18] Its Cairo correspondent reported: 'In Arab countries generally, the ultra-radical
fringe has seemed to be shrinking. Most Arab governments have
long since recognized the threat it poses. Concerted and often
brutal policing has decapitated most of the extreme groups. Some
organizations that were once considered dangerously radical, such
as Lebanon's Shia militia, Hizbullah, have moved into the mainstream. Even Egypt's Gamaa Islamiya, an organization that
wrought havoc in the early 1990s, has renounced violence,
although its jailed leader has since wavered. *To most Muslims, the
contention of Osama bin Laden and his followers that God has ordered
Muslims to kill Americans is not only silly, but presumption bordering on
heresy.*'

How 'Muslim' or how 'Arab', then, was bin Laden's crime?
The journal was simply unprepared to face the issue squarely. Its
editorial, on October 13, lapsed into disgraceful escapism. It was
entitled, provocatively: 'Muslims and the West: The need to speak
up'. The theme was Orientalism pure and simple in the good
Huntington manner: 'Militant Islam despises the West not for
what it does but for what it is. . . . The truth is, America is
despised mainly for its success, for the appealing and, critics would
say, corrupting alternatives it presents to a traditional Islamic way
of life; and for the humiliation which many Muslims feel when
they consider the comparative failure, in material terms, of their
once-mighty civilization'. The same issue carried a report by the

Cairo correspondent quoting the president of Al-Azhar Islamic University, 'a bastion of moderate Muslim orthodoxy'. No admirer of bin Laden, he said: 'There will be no stability, and no end to terrorism, so long as the Palestinian people are under occupation'. He was not advocating terrorism, only pointing out its prime cause in West Asia. *The Economist* itself recognized that 'one *cause celebre* in Arab minds is, *naturally*, Israel'.[19]

Except among a few, there is no understanding in the West of the depth of, and justification for, the anger. Edward W. Said, Professor of English and Comparative Literature at Columbia University, recalled the British writer Edward J. Thompson's book *The Other Side of the Medal* (1926), which pointed out how British writings on India 'simply left out the Indian side of things'. They dilated on the terrorist movement in India but studiously ignored its causes – British repression and denial of India's aspiration to independence. 'Change Thompson's context and time, substitute "peace process" for "Reforms", Palestinians and Arabs for Indians, and Israelis for British, and you have an accurate account of the present impasse. Great, deliberately bloody and indiscriminately violent actions like the 1857 Mutiny or the recent bombings in Jerusalem and Tel Aviv are ugly, indefensible things; they sacrifice the lives of Israelis and Palestinians as they did Indians and Europeans; they induce more hatred and feelings of revenge. . . . But there has been little more obdurate and arrogant than the Israeli and American response, with its sanctimonious choruses against terrorism, Hamas, Islamic fundamentalism, and its equally odious hymns to peacemaking, the peace process, and the peace of the brave. The grotesque display of bad faith, graceless posturing and, for Clinton and Peres, brazen electioneering that was the Sharm el Sheikh summit simply made the contradictions even more glaring. Here were Israel and the United States, whose military record of imperialist behavior in the postwar world is virtually unrivaled for its lawlessness, wrapping themselves in the mantle of moralism and self-congratulation.'[20]

Said, a Christian Palestinian, gives short shrift to those who regard Islam and the West as watertight categories in which every Westerner and every Muslim is somehow completely at one with his respective civilizational category. Neither is homogenous.

'Islam of course is a religion, but it is also a culture: the Arabic language is the same for Muslims as it is for Christians, both of whom, believers and non-believers alike, are deeply affected – perhaps the better word is inflected – by the Quran, which is also in Arabic.

'There are of course distinctly Christian traditions inside the Islamic world. I myself belong to one. But it would be grossly inaccurate to think of them as separate and outside Islam, which includes us all. This, I think, is the most important point of all; Islam is something all Arabs share in, and is an integral part of our identity. I know that I may be speaking only for myself when I say that as an Arab Christian I have never felt myself to be a member of an aggrieved or marginal minority. Being an Arab, even for a non-Muslim, means being a member of what the late Marshal Hodgson called an Islamicate world, or culture. Any attempts at severing the tie are, I believe, doomed to failure.'[21]

This explains why the response of the famous Lebanese diplomat, Charles H. Malik, the militant Georges Habash and the intellectual Edward Said to Israel's establishment was no different from that of their Muslim Arab compatriots. It is one of the most monstrous wrongs committed in human history. Americans simply refuse to understand that. An increasingly large number of Israelis and not a few Europeans do though.

Arnold Hottinger, correspondent for the *Neue Zurcher Zeitung* from 1956 to 1991, summed up the reason for Arab resentment with succinct accuracy: 'Arab resentment against the West *predates the rise of Islamism by a long time*. For about 20 years after the beginning of independence and the founding of Israel this resentment was channeled into *Arab nationalism*, mostly of the pan-Arab variety. There is little doubt that the newly formed state of Israel was the catalyst for such feelings of ill will. People from outside the Middle East were allowed to take hold of an Arab country and expel a large part of its indigenous population – in spite of declarations by Arab leadership that this would never happen and in spite of their strenuous attempts to prevent this development by diplomatic and military means. The creation of Israel against Arab will and what they considered elementary justice rankled all the more because at the time Arab states had just become independent or were working toward that status. Independence had already been promised to them during World War I and again to most of them during World War II. But there was one Arab country that was deprived of independence and forced to submit to the immigrant Westerners who proclaimed themselves the true owners of the land. There was no means, not even resorting to war, that could undo what was seen as a clear injustice to the Palestinians and with them Arabs at large.

'There were many more reasons for Arab resentment against the West, but they were more or less temporary. Colonialism and Western domination eventually ceased. Other difficulties, misunderstandings and contradictions were overcome. But Israeli presence remained and was reinforced over the years.'[22]

Yet, Israel's Prime Minister Yitzak Rabin had no qualms about claiming, 'We stand first today in the line of fire against the danger of extremist Islam' – not Arab nationalism. Contrast this with what Israel's Acting Foreign Minister, Shlomo Ben Ami, said. Akina Eldar reported in a leading daily *Haaretz*, on November 28, 2000, a statement which Ben Ami made in the course of a Cabinet debate over a document prepared by the Prime Minister's office. It purported to catalogue a long list of Palestinian transgressions. Ben Ami opposed the distribution of the document on the ground that no one in the West would be surprised that a people under occupation fails to honour agreements with its occupier: 'Accusations made by a well established society about how a people it is oppressing is breaking rules to attain its rights do not have much credence'.

There is a school of revisionist historians in Israel, steeped in learning and inspired by a passionate commitment to historical truth. Ilan Pappé, a Haifa University scholar, is the most outspoken among them. In an interview with Dan Perry of the Associated Press, he gave a resounding 'Yes' to the question, 'Was Israel born in sin?' He amplified: 'The Jews came and took, by means of uprooting and expulsion, a land that was Arab. . . . We wanted to be a colonialist occupier, and yet to come across as moral at the same time'.[23] Can such a gross outrage ever be condoned? Palestine had been under Muslim rule for seven centuries.[24]

Tom Segev, an Israeli journalist and historian, has documented in a book how force and fraud were systematically employed by the British rulers of Palestine from 1919 to 1948 to establish Jewish rule, in complicity with Zionist leaders.[25] The author's research led him to an interesting encounter: 'The Zionist movement made great efforts to establish a link with Gandhi to garner his support. Gandhi expressed his sympathy for the persecuted Jews in Nazi Germany but rejected the Zionist programme, partly because it involved the use of British force against the Arabs. He expressed a qualified understanding for Arab terrorism and suggested that the Jews of Palestine not fight the Arabs even if they tried to throw them into the Dead Sea; the world's sympathy would save the Jews in the end, he believed. In turn, Ben-Gurion made some non-committal statement about the liberation of India. Just as Gandhi could not support Zionism because he opposed British rule in his country, so Ben-Gurion could not support freedom for India because he favoured the continuation of British rule in Palestine'.

Segev further records: 'The Zionist Organization and the British government continued to bribe influential Arabs. President Roosevelt told Chaim Weizmann that, in his opinion, the Arabs could be bought. . . . In the minutes of their conversation the Arab word "*baksheesh*" appears. The Jewish Agency's biggest client seems to have been Prince Abdullah of Transjordan'.[26]

Arab wrath is directed against their own corrupt leaders no less than against the United States, Britain, and the state they planted in the Arab world – Israel. 'Those bomb throwers and wild men are the result of an almost unimaginably corrupt and mediocre government', Nasser's confidant and one of the most astute commentators on the Arab world, Muhammad Hassanein Heikal, said.

It is these very corrupt despots whom the USA propped up all through the Cold War, and supports still. The USA was uncomfortable with secularists like Nasser. It preferred dictators like Zia-ul-Haq who used the cry of Islamization to legitimize his usurpation of power in Pakistan in 1977. The noted writer Shabbir Akhtar angrily recalled:

'Much of the current opposition to democracy in Islamic lands comes directly from Western government policy rather than from the activities of those omnipresent villains, the Muslim fundamentalists.

'Several repressive regimes in the Islamic world are actively supported by Western powers, particularly the USA, Britain and France. The CIA continues to help many a tyrant. The Americans and the British befriended the Shah of Iran. Saddam Hussein was a friend of the democratic West until he raped Kuwait and his Western admirers decided to revise their definitions of good and evil. The French have encouraged many pro-Western dictatorships in North Africa. There are only dependent and independent dictatorships in the House of Islam; and the West supports the dependent ones. Is it, then, in the interests of Western powers even to allow, let alone encourage, democracy on Islamic soil? . . . We Muslims rightly resent the West's interference in Islamic affairs, its determined attempts to place Westerners and their fellow "Muslim" conspirators at the helm of our political destinies. Britain and America have no right to arrange peace conferences to decide our fate: the House of Islam is not an American protectorate.'[27]

'The fundamentalists' who rose in revolt differed from one another as much as the despots. There was nothing in common between Zia-ul-Haq, who encouraged the ulama (clergy), and Libya's Muammar Gaddafi, who denounced the ulama as 'reactionaries', rejected their interpretation of Islam and denied the authenticity of many prophetic traditions (hadith). In Palestine alone, two militant bodies, Hamas and Islamic Jihad, oppose each other on crucial points. The Jihad movement in the Central Asian Republics of Uzbekistan and Tajikistan has different motivations from those that drive, say, Hamas or Islamic Jihad in Palestine.

Ancient animosities, modern hate

September 11, 2001, changed a lot. Suddenly American security became linked to events in Asia. The Taliban regime is destroyed; but at a very heavy cost of human lives. Bin Laden's fate, at the time of writing, is not known. In the long run, however, the war against such forces can be won only by winning the hearts and minds of the people. There is little sign of such an effort by the United States. On December 15, 2001, even as the war was raging in Afghanistan, the US vetoed a Security Council resolution condemning 'acts of terror' against Israelis and Palestinians and demanding an end to nearly 15 months of violence in the region. It was supported by 12 of the 15 members of the Council, with Britain and Norway abstaining. The US Ambassador, John

Negroponte, told the Council that the resolution aimed to 'isolate politically one of the parties to the conflict through an attempt to throw the weight of the Council behind the other party'. This pro-Israeli tilt will continue and so will the prejudices of old for quite some time to come.

September 11 brought those prejudices to the fore in the West. It also helped hate-mongers in India to jump on the American bandwagon. There is, however, a fundamental difference between the prejudice against Muslims in the West and the hostility towards them in India. Thirteen centuries ossified Western prejudice. In India the prejudice against Muslims is only about a century old; it is most certainly not ancient. It is *modern* hate retailed by the fascist RSS (Rashtriya Swayamsevak Sangh) whose political wing, the BJP, is the dominant partner in the National Democratic Alliance which rules India today.[28]

Susanne Hoeber Rudolph and Lloyd I. Rudolph convincingly demonstrated 'how ancient animosities get invented' in an article entitled 'Modern Hate', shortly after the demolition of the Babri mosque. The question they posed was why traditionally harmonious mosaics in India were shattered. '"Ancient hatreds" are thus made as much as they are inherited. To call them ancient is to pretend they are primordial forces, outside of history and human agency, when often they are merely synthetic antiques. Intellectuals, writers, artists and politicians "make" hatreds. Films and videos, texts and textbooks, certify stories about the past, the collective memories that shape perceptions and attitudes. . . . L.K. Advani told India's electorate that if the countries of Western Europe and the United States can call themselves Christian, India should be free to call itself Hindu.

'One of the ways to think about the recent savaging of the Babri Masjid by young Hindu men is to see it as a re-negotiation of political and economic power and status, or rather as a sign of the pathology of re-negotiation.'

Referring to the controversy over reservations, they recall Advani's Rath Yatra and how he 'had succeeded in polarizing Indian politics on communal rather than caste-class lines'. The writers conclude: 'When TV talking heads and oped contributors portray "mobs" as "frenzied" and believers as "fanatic", they have given up the task of discerning the human inducements and political calculations that make politics happen. They have given up making motives visible and showing how they are transformed. "Ancient hatreds" function like the "evil empire". That term, too, was a projection on a screen, obscuring the motives and practice that lay behind it. The doctrine of ancient hatreds may become the post-Cold War's most robust mystification, in a way of having an enemy and knowing evil that deceives as it satisfies. The hatred is modern, and may be closer than we think'.[29]

Cashing in on the attack on the WTC, the RSS supremo, K.S. Sudarshan, expatiated on October 26, 2001, on the RSS's notions of Islam and Christianity: 'Religious texts contain different messages given in different contexts. The main question is, to which of these messages you give importance and how you interpret them'. He then goes on to quote from the Quran and the Bible, claiming to show how Muslims and Christians have selectively used their scripture to 'take to the path of intolerance and conflict. So far, history shows that most of them have opted for the route of intolerance and conflict only. That is why the history of Christianity and Islam is soaked in bloodshed'.[30] The Quranic verses which Sudarshan cited will be discussed fully in chapter 3 on jihad. For the moment, let us only note that his charges merely reflected the outlook which his influential predecessor, M.S. Golwalkar, articulated in his book *Bunch of Thoughts* (1966), the RSS bible: 'They [Muslims] came here as invaders. . . . History has recorded that their antagonism was not merely political. . . . But it was so deep-rooted that whatever the Hindu believed in, the Muslim was wholly hostile to it. If we worship in the temple he would desecrate it. If we carry on [sic] bhajans [devotional songs] and car [sic] festivals, that would irritate him. If we worship cow, he would like to eat it. If we glorify woman as a symbol of sacred motherhood, he would like to molest it. He was tooth and nail opposed to our way of life in all aspects – religious, cultural, social etc'.[31] Sudarshan himself said on April 27, 1991: 'If Muslims have to stay in India they will have to submit to the Indianization [read: Hinduization] of their religion. . . . preserving only the essential 10 per cent and do away with the other 90 per cent of their religion, incorporating in its stead elements of the Indian culture'.[32]

Four distinguished scholars have exposed these myths as well as the modernity of their coinage. 'The myth of the Muslim invader and Hindu resistance has also been deployed to prove that Hindutva represents the true, native nationalism. It may be conceded that there is an area of overlap in ideas and personnel between Hindu communalism and mainstream nationalism. The communalism of the majority community, Nehru once pointed out, can easily pass off as national, while that of the minorities is quickly branded as separatist. It is well known, for instance, that the myth of medieval "Muslim tyranny" and Hindu (particularly Rajput, Maratha and Sikh) "National" resistance *was developed or endorsed in the late nineteenth century by many of the acknowledged founding fathers of Indian nationalism*: Bankimchandra would only be the most obvious example of this phenomenon.'[33]

While Western leaders are at pains to emphasize that theirs is not a fight against Islam, the RSS is out to denigrate Islam itself. An RSS ideologue, Ram Swarup, has written pamphlets entitled *Hindu View of Christianity and Islam*; another, Sita Ram Goel, has written *Jesus Christ: An Artifice for Aggression*, which accused Christians of branding the Jews as killers of Jesus Christ. Ram Swarup brands Islam as a religion which 'teaches to kill the un-believers'.

The historian Romila Thapar has in her writings nailed to the counter the lies about the religious divide in history: 'The need for postulating a Hindu community became a requirement for political mobilization *in the nineteenth century*' as a key to power.[34] Fortunately, there has been a similar effort in the West to expose the falsehoods about Islam and the Muslims which have been readily accepted by scholars, poets, theologians, historians and by very many others for centuries, and have moulded a climate of opinion which the modern media faithfully reflect.

Meanwhile, the Spectre of Islam continues to haunt very many in the media, in academia, in the arts and in scholarship. Few care to free themselves from its thrall. Those in the West who have, have rendered high service to the truth by their ceaseless exposition of Islam's message and its history. The present writer is deeply indebted to them. This is a modest effort in the same direction, drawing on the works of scholars of distinction, and inviting the reader to explore for himself the enormous field of research mapped out in those works.

Plan of the book

The following chapter, 'The Long March of Prejudice', assesses the burden of history and points to its continuing impact on the media today. For good or ill, Western media set the tone for the rest of the world to follow. Islamophobes in the West have their counterparts elsewhere; in India particularly, for historical reasons.

Even writings which profess to clear up the cobwebs that surround jihad and fatwa end up by adopting familiar notions. The conduct of Muslim rulers in the past is depicted as Islam in action. It is trite to say that the faith was given by God while man shapes history. Men who profess to act in the name of the faith do not necessarily represent it. It is shoddy scholarship to regard it otherwise. This, of course, is true of all faiths; indeed, of all ideologies as well.

Chapter 3, 'The Meanings of Jihad and Fatwa', argues that jihad in Islam is far removed from the jihad waged in the name of Islam throughout the centuries, right down to Osama Bin Laden. Fatwa, a legal opinion, became an edict for use by clerics as a weapon of oppression in the service of the ruler of the day or a tool in the trade for personal gain.

What has come to be known as Islamic Fundamentalism must be viewed in a historical context, and in the light of similar movements in other faiths. Its political failure was apparent even before September 11, 2001, as the great authority, Professor Olivier Roy, pointed out well before the tragedy. As chapter 4, 'The Very Modern Roots of Islamic Fundamentalism', records, events since have vindicated him.

It is, however, not enough to dispel wrong notions. It is vastly more important to draw on the considerable corpus of the faith which has a profound relevance to our times. Chapter 5, 'Human Rights in the Islamic Tradition', attempts to do this. It demonstrates how human rights and a theology of liberation are firmly rooted in the Quran and the teachings of Prophet Muhammad.

Related to this is the pressing and inescapable challenge facing Muslims the world over: the challenge of modernity. This is explored in the concluding chapter, 'Ijtihad (Reason) and the Challenge of Modernity'. The space has been monopolized by the fundamentalist. His appeal to the masses exploits the insecurities which their situations, in diverse conditions, instill in them. The liberal Muslim receives far less attention. In Islam, ijtihad equips and empowers the Muslim to face the challenge of modernity. This tradition, spanning a little over the last century in South Asia alone, from Syed Ahmad Khan to Chiragh Ali, Iqbal and more recently, Fazlur Rehman, is impressive. It must be revived.

CHAPTER 2

THE LONG MARCH
OF PREJUDICE

'A victorious line of march had been prolonged above a thousand miles from the rock of Gibraltar to the banks of the Loire; the repetition of an equal space would have carried the Saracens to the confines of Poland and the Highlands of Scotland; the Rhine is not more impassable than the Nile or Euphrates and the Arabian fleet might have sailed without a naval combat into the mouth of the Thames. Perhaps the interpretation of the Koran would now be taught in the schools of Oxford, and her pulpits might demonstrate to a circumcised people the sanctity and truth of the revelation of Muhammad.'[1]

Edward Gibbon was relieved that 'from such calamities was Christendom delivered by the genius and fortune of one man', Charles Martel. He defeated at Poitiers (Tours) in 732 the forces of Abd al-Rahman whose detachments had overspread the kingdom of Burgundy as far as the cities of Lyons and Besançon. The first Arab invasion of France was conducted in 718. A few years after their defeat in 732, not far from Paris, they returned in force to France. Maurontius, the duke of Marseilles, had allied himself with the Arabs. By 759 their expulsion from France was complete. Over a thousand years later, Gibbon re-lived the events in statuesque prose. His magnum opus, *The Decline and Fall of the Roman Empire*, was published in 1781. History is an intoxicant. Military operations and empires leave in their train a corpus of myths, legends and bitter memories that linger. Christendom launched seven Crusades against Muslim rulers over 175 years, from 1095 to 1270. During the Prophet's lifetime, Islam was confined to the Arabian Peninsula. He died in 632, and soon after that, Islam spread with extraordinary rapidity. Persia, Syria, Egypt,

Turkey and North Africa fell to Arab forces. In the eighth and ninth centuries, Spain, Sicily and parts of France were conquered. By the thirteenth and fourteenth centuries, Muslims ruled in India, Indonesia and China. The Arab Empire gradually declined. Baghdad fell to the Mongols in 1055. In Spain the Christian Reconquista movement extinguished Arab rule by conquering the last stronghold, Granada, in 1492. Arab rule in Spain lasted for nearly eight centuries. However, in 1453 Constantinople fell to the forces of Sultan Mehmed II. In the eyes of Europe, the Turks had taken over from the Arabs as 'the Islamic threat to Christian Europe'. Having conquered Egypt in 1517, the Turks reached the gates of Vienna twice, in 1529 and in 1683, but were repulsed. For five hundred years the Ottomans were Europe's most feared enemy.

In the first decade of the nineteenth century, the Ottoman Empire spread across North Africa, the Arabian Peninsula, Iraq, Syria, Lebanon and the greater part of the Balkans as far as the lower reaches of the Danube. It also included Palestine. Muslims conquered Jerusalem in 638. The Ottoman Empire was liquidated in 1919 immediately after the First World War. It had supported the wrong side in the war, the Germans. The British acquired a Mandate to rule over Palestine from the League of Nations and went to work. The Arab provinces of the Ottoman Empire were split between Britain and France. Britain became responsible for Palestine, to be ruled directly, and Iraq through a monarch; France became responsible for Syria and Lebanon. A principality of Transjordan was established. In 1948 the Jewish State of Israel was established on Arab land, with American support, and through terror.

The burden of history

What has this history to do with the image of Islam in modern times? Minou Reeves explains its relevance with a wealth of documentation. Until 1979 she was an Iranian career diplomat; yet she harbours not a trace of the bitterness which members of the *ancien régime* have for the new order. Married to Prof. Nigel Reeves, she is a Fellow of the Institute of Linguistics in London. Her book, *Muhammad in Europe*,[2] is a work of high scholarship which surveys, with copious quotations backed by full references, over a millennium's record of European denigration of Muhammad. It left its mark on the minds of the West as well as the Arab world.

To come to the immediate issue of Palestine, Minou records: 'On his arrival in Jerusalem [in 1917] General Allenby made a historic remark which indicated that the long-standing animosity between Christendom and Islam was not over and that the crusading mentality was still alive. Speaking in public, he announced that the crusades were now finally completed. And three years later, in 1920, when French troops occupied Damascus, their commander marched up to Saladin's tomb in the Great Mosque and cried: "Nous revenons, Saladin" (We are back, Saladin). The deep-seated contempt for Islam had long displayed itself amongst the French colonialists as a sense of vindictiveness towards the Muslim populations of the former Ottoman Empire'.[3]

The British were no better. There were only 60,000 Jews in Palestine at that time as against 750,000 Muslims, mostly Arabs. But the British Foreign Secretary A.J. Balfour wrote in 1918: 'The four Great Powers are *committed* to Zionism and Zionism, be it right or wrong, good or bad, is rooted in age-long tradition, in present needs, in future hopes, of far profounder import than the desires and prejudices of the 700,000 Arabs who now inhabit that ancient land'.[4]

Reeves rightly remarks: 'The modern conflict between Muslims and Jews was triggered by Western colonial dictates and by Zionism. It radicalized Islam and divorced it once again, as in the Medieval Ages, from its mother-faiths, Judaism and Christianity.

Islam had been forced into isolation, provoking anti-European feelings amongst its followers. The Balfour Declaration had reinforced the Jewish people's awareness of its ancient claim, rooted in the religious history of Israel and the destruction of its state by the Romans in A.D. 70 . . . [T]he first Jewish-Muslim territorial and ideological conflict since the advent of Islam . . . was in the making'.

Today, Israel is reluctant to permit an independent Palestinian State on a mere one-third of that land. The sensitivities of the entire Muslim world have been inflamed by Israel's brutal repression and expansionism. In the past, Islamic revivalism was a reaction to Western colonialism. Secular Pan-Arabism was undermined by Western support to corrupt Arab rulers who supported or acquiesced in the West's policies. What passes for Islamic fundamentalism today received a boost with the West's establishment of Israel on Arab soil, and Israeli expansion. The noted scholar Leone Caetani saw it coming and warned as early in 1919: 'The convulsion has shaken Islamic and Oriental civilization to its foundations. The entire Oriental world, from China to the Mediterranean, is in ferment. Everywhere the hidden fire of anti-European hatred is burning. Riots in Morocco, risings in Algiers, discontent in Tripoli, so-called nationalist attempts in Egypt, Arabia, and Libya are different manifestations of the same deep sentiment and have as their objective the rebellion of the Oriental world against European civilization.

'The principal reason for this ferment is the report spread throughout the world that the Entente wishes to suppress the Ottoman Empire, dividing its territory among the powers *and ceding Palestine to the Jews.*'[5]

Minou Reeves writes: 'Over the course of no less than thirteen centuries a stubbornly biased and consistently negative outlook had persisted, permeating deep levels of European consciousness. In the works of an overwhelming majority of European writers Muhammad was portrayed as a man of deep moral

faults. Churchmen, historians, orientalists, biographers, philoso-
phers, dramatists, poets and politicians alike had sought to
attribute to Islam and especially to Muhammad fanatical and
disreputable, even demonic characteristics'.

Thirteen centuries of calumny have moulded the West's
perception of Islam. Muslims reacted first by apologetics; later, by
denunciation of the West. Political developments shaped the
response. It was bad enough to be colonized; worse still, to be
despised by the rulers. Indians are not strangers to English historiography, which contributed a lot to deepening the communal
divide in the country. The Babri mosque question originated in
false allegations of Babar's destruction of a temple made by an
English official, Patrick Carnegy of the Bengal Civil Service, in
1860, as the historian Sushil Srivastava has established.[6]

Minou Reeves does not condone Muslim fundamentalism
nor does she ignore the services rendered by Western scholars to
Islamic history and theology. 'Coming closer to the present day, it
becomes plain to see how these images, so deeply rooted in the
Western consciousness, have helped to ignite the suspicion and
resentment towards the West that manifests itself in Islamic
Fundamentalism. Far from being a recent phenomenon, this
emerged in response to European colonialism in the Islamic
Orient from North Africa to Indonesia, and most crucially to the
establishment of Israel in the heart of the Near East.

'Today the attraction of Islamic Fundamentalism reaches
beyond revolutionary Iran, to Turkey, Egypt, and dramatically
close to Europe – to Algeria. Its impact has been so great in recent
years that, even as more balanced pictures of Muhammad and his
religion have begun to appear in Western writings, they have been
eclipsed by images of a radical, anti-Western and violent Islam that
once again bears the hallmarks of the age-old prejudices. It is as if
the wheel of history has turned full circle back to the age of the
Crusade and Holy Wars.'

Intellectual stagnation in the Muslim world

Islam was not only a military threat to Europe but also an ideological and moral challenge because it enunciated an alternative
vision. In intellectual and cultural spheres the Arab world could
mock Europe. 'The Islamic world was far ahead of the Christian
West in medicine, mathematics and in some aspects of physics
such as optics, in astronomy, chemistry, botany and other natural
sciences. With the adoption of the Indian zero, the Arabs had
greatly simplified arithmetical exercises and had developed new
disciplines in mathematics such as algebra, analytical geometry and
spherical trigonometry. Until 1600 the chief medical textbook in
Europe was the *Canon of Medicine* of Avicenna, an eleventh-
century Persian scientist and philosopher whose homeland had
become part of the rapidly expanding Islamic Empire. The Arabs
established colleges of translation in Spain and Sicily which made
the wealth of knowledge in Greek, Syriac, Persian and Sanskrit
writings, available in Arabic. They were in turn translated into
Latin. Great halls of science with libraries and astronomical labora-
tories were created alongside the translation colleges to promote
research. Spain and Sicily thus became two major centres for
intellectual and scientific exchange between East and West, con-
tributing significantly to the emergence of European Humanism
and the Renaissance.

'But how could these Bedouin men of the desert, whose civilization had begun in tribalism, achieve such high levels of
sophistication and knowledge in such a short time? The answer is
simple. The freshness of the new religion had enabled the Arabs
to extend their faith beyond the boundaries of the Arabian
Peninsula into the highly civilized world of the Persians, the
Greeks and the Byzantines. They had inherited the dazzling
riches of Persian and Greek philosophies and had been remark-
ably apt in imitating the courtly manners, habits and traditions of

the Persian nobility, aspects of which they introduced to southern Europe. The Europeans thus became more and more convinced of the superiority of Muslim culture, which made them envious and resentful. Consequently, Muhammad as the initiator and inspirer of this ever-growing success began to haunt them in all walks of life.'[7]

Muslims would do well to reflect why Europe, which had borrowed a lot from them, forged ahead, while Muslim states stagnated. Historically, the intellectual stagnation in the Muslim world *preceded* Western colonialism and made resistance to its march difficult. In the West, the campaign of calumny of Islam and its Prophet Muhammad, which had begun when the Muslim world was resurgent, did not stop as Europe gained ascendancy. It acquired a sharper edge and greater assurance which, in turn, fuelled Muslim anger.

Minou Reeves's survey of Western writings is meticulously detailed right from the days of the Biblical scholar the Venerable Bede, who died in 735, to this day. Medieval Europe's fear of Islam drove it to demonizing Muhammad. 'The name Mahound or sometimes Mahoun, Mahun, Mahomet, in French Mahon, in German Machmet, which was synonymous with demon, devil, idol, was invented by the writers of Christian play cycles and romances of twelfth century Europe. In these writings Muhammad does not appear as a prophet or even anti-prophet, but as a heathen idol worshipped by the Arabs.'

Some of the most highly regarded poets and scholars contributed to the campaign. Chaucer's *Canterbury Tales* (1476) was mild in comparison to Dante's *Divine Comedy*. When Dante was writing at the close of the Middle Ages in the early 1300s in Florence, Islam still appeared as a major threat from the East. 'The Christian West was planning further crusading expeditions to counteract the peril which Islam presented. In 1291, some twenty years before Dante began the *Divine Comedy*, the last Crusaders' fortress, Acre, in Palestine had been reconquered by the Muslims who had driven the Crusaders from the region. The images of those wars were vivid in Dante's mind when he created the ugly portrait of Muhammad in his *Inferno*. Dante consigned Muhammad and his disciple Ali, with their bodies split from head to waist, to the eighth circle of Hell. The poet portrays Muhammad as a sinner tearing apart his severed breast with his own hands, a symbolic gesture to show that he was the chief among the damned souls to have brought schism into religion. For Dante, Muhammad's crime had been to propagate a "false religion", to deliver a divine revelation claiming to supersede Christianity, which had to be regarded as an impious fraud and which could only sow discord in the world.'[8]

In all history, no other religion has been treated to such a sustained flow of calumny; no other founder of religion to such vile and sustained denigration. The Renaissance and Reformation in Europe made not the slightest difference. Nor did progress in scholarship, greater curiosity about, and even goodwill towards, the East.

Karen Armstrong's perception of Western attitudes and the Muslims' reaction is similar to that of Minou Reeves. She spent seven years as a Roman Catholic nun before embarking on a research degree at Oxford, taught at a girls' school and became a full-time writer and broadcaster. Her book, *Muhammad: A Biography of the Prophet*,[9] is more than a work of erudition. It is a feat of deep insight into a faith other than one's own. She notes how the West responded warmly to teachers like S. Radhakrishnan: 'The barriers of geographical distance, hostility and fear, which once kept the religions in separate watertight compartments, are beginning to fall. . . . But one major religion seems to be outside this circle of goodwill and, in the West at least, to have retained its negative image. People who are beginning to find inspiration in Zen or Taoism are usually not nearly so eager to look kindly upon Islam, even though it is the third religion of

Abraham and more in tune with our own Judaeo-Christian tradition. In the West we have a long history of hostility towards Islam that seems as entrenched as our anti-Semitism. . . . But the old hatred of Islam continues to flourish on both sides of the Atlantic and people have few scruples about attacking this religion, even if they know little about it.

'The hostility is understandable, because until the rise of the Soviet Union in our own century, no polity or ideology posed such a continuous challenge to the West as Islam.'[10]

In his much acclaimed *Tamberlaine* (1590), Christopher Marlowe had Tamberlaine order his soldiers to burn the Quran before his eyes as a token of his victory over the Turks:

> *In vain, I see, men worship Mahomet:*
> *My sword hath sent millions of Turks to hell,*
> *Slew all his priests, his kinsmen, and his friend:*
> *And yet I live untouched by Mahomet.*
> *There is a God full of revenging wrath,*
> *From whom the thunder and the lightening breaks,*
> *Whose scourge I am, and him will I obey.*
> *So Casane, fling them in the fire.*[11]

Martin Luther's revolt against the Pope did not diminish his vituperation of Prophet Muhammad: 'The Turk kills the body and plunders and lays waste the property of Christians, but the Pope stresses his Quran far more cruelly, in order that Christ may be denied. Both, of course, are the enemies of the Church and the Devil's own slaves, because both reject the Gospel'.

Milton, Voltaire, Montesquieu, Diderot, Victor Hugo, Byron, Shelley and Thackeray contributed their mite, men of acknowledged stature who moulded European thought and sentiment and also buttressed Europe's age-old antipathy towards Islam. This was well after Muslim power had ceased to be a military threat to Europe and the Ottoman Empire had become 'the Sick Man of Europe'.

There is another tradition whose contribution Minou Reeves acknowledges unstintedly – 'the tradition of Roger Bacon, of John of Segovia, of Lessing, of young Goethe, of Boulain-villiers, of Bolingbroke, of Carlyle, of Dawson, of Reland, of Rilke, of Paret, of Sprenger, of Tor Andrae, of Bodley, of Montgomery Watt, of Rodinson, of Annemarie Schimmel. They have sought to understand Muhammad's cause, Muhammad's message, Muhammad's social and political reforms, Muhammad's personality and character in the context of his times and with an open mind. They have sought to dispel the myths and the stereotypes and to show how Islam embraces values dear to religions that have regarded it as their sworn enemy, while Muhammad himself saw his Faith as the continuation and enhancement of those very religions'.[12]

Is everything Muslim 'Islamic'?

It is not only the popular mind that treats any occurrence of mishap or misfortune in an Arab or Muslim country as an 'Islamic' event. Reputed scholars of Islam share the same mindset. As Edward Said writes in his seminal work, *Orientalism*: 'In page after page of [Sir Hamilton] Gibb's prose in *Whither Islam?* we learn that the new commercial banks in Egypt and Syria are facts of Islam or an Islamic initiative; schools and an increasing literacy rate are Islamic facts too, as are journalism, Westernization, and intellectual societies. At no point does Gibb speak of European colonialism when he discusses the rise of nationalism and its "toxins". That the history of modern Islam might be more intelligible for its resistance, political and nonpolitical, to colonialism, never occurs to Gibb, just as it seems to him finally irrelevant to note whether the "Islamic" governments he discusses are republican, feudal, or monarchical.

'"Islam" for Gibb is a sort of superstructure imperilled both by politics (nationalism, communist agitation, Westernization) and by dangerous Muslim attempts to tamper with its intellectual sovereignty.'[13]

But one must turn to Said's more recent work, *Covering Islam*, for a thorough exposure of such scholarship and of the media: 'Why is it that a whole range of political, cultural, social, and even economic events has often seemed reducible in so Pavlovian a way to "Islam"? What is it about "Islam" that provokes so quick and unrestrained a response? In what way do "Islam" and the Islamic world differ for Westerners from, say, the rest of the Third World and, during the Cold War, the Soviet Union?'[14]

One scholar deserves special notice: Bernard Lewis. More than any other modern scholar, it is he who has done most to project the stereotypical image of Islam and Muslims as menacing militant fundamentalists. He published a chapter called 'The Revolt of Islam' in a book in 1964, then republished much of the same material twelve years later, slightly altered to suit the new place of publication and retitled 'The Return of Islam'.[15]

Lewis' article 'The Roots of Muslim Rage' propounded the same thesis as Samuel P. Huntington's more famous 'The Clash of Civilizations'.[16] As Esposito noted, 'The message and impact of "The Roots of Muslim Rage" is reinforced by the picture on the front cover of the *Atlantic Monthly*, portraying a scowling, bearded, turbaned Muslim with American flags in his glaring eyes. The threat motif and confrontational tone are supplemented by the two pictures used in the article, ostensibly presenting the quintessential Muslim perception of America as the enemy. The first is of a serpent marked with the stars and stripes seen crossing a desert (America's dominance of or threat to the Arab world); the second shows the serpent poised as if to attack from behind an unsuspecting pious Muslim at prayer. Like other sensationalist stereotypes, pictures meant to be provocative, to attract the reader, feed into our ignorance and reinforce a myopic vision of the reality. Muslims are attired in "traditional" dress, bearded and turbaned, despite the fact that most Muslims (and most "fundamentalists") do not dress or look like this. The result reinforces the image of Islamic activists as medieval in life-style and mentality'.[17]

No wonder the scholar Ziauddin Sardar dubbed Bernard Lewis 'a senior statesman of Zionist historiography'.[18] Imagine the credence a Lewis will receive, say, in India, among the unwary. He has written on the Arabs and on Islam for over half a century and scaled heights in academia in his own country, Britain, and recently in the United States. His essay, 'The Roots of Muslim Rage', perfectly justifies Edward Said's devastating censure. 'To call what Lewis does in this extremely influential essay either scholarship or interpretation is to travesty the meaning of both.' 'The Roots of Muslim Rage' is a crude polemic devoid of historical truth, rational argument, or human wisdom. It attempts to characterize Muslims as one terrifyingly collective person enraged at an outside world that has disturbed his almost primeval calm and unchallenged rule. For example: '[T]he last straw was the challenge to his [the putative Muslim's] mastery in his own house, from emancipated women and rebellious children. It was too much to endure, and the outbreak of rage against these alien, infidel, and incomprehensible forces that had subverted his [sic] dominance, disrupted his society, and finally violated the sanctuary of his society was inevitable. It was also natural that this rage should be directed primarily against the millennial enemy and should draw its strength from ancient beliefs and loyalties.

'Later Lewis contradicts himself by saying that Muslims had once welcomed the West, responding to it "with admiration and emulation". But this he alleges dissolves into pure hatred and rage "when the deeper passions are stirred", seemingly with only those inner feelings to blame for such unseemly outbursts.'[19]

However the *pièce de resistance* in the book *Covering Islam* is the chapter on 'Islam as News'. The Islamic Revolution in Iran in February 1979 shook the West, particularly the United States, which lost a staunch ally, the Shah, and found in his place a government with a mind of its own. The jihad motif received wide currency. In an article in *Chicago Tribune*[20] Roy Moseley accused Ayatollah Khomeini of unleashing 'a holy war on the world'. Jihad became the single most important motif in Western comment. Edmund Bosworth argued in the *Los Angeles Times* on December 12, 1979 that 'all political activity for a period of about twelve hundred years in an area that includes Turkey, Iran, Sudan, Ethiopia, Spain, and India can be understood as emanating from the Muslim call for a jihad'.[21]

In many instances, 'Islam' licensed not only patent inaccuracy but also expressions of unrestrained ethnocentrism, cultural, and even racial, hatred, deep yet paradoxically free-floating hostility. All this took place as part of what is presumed to be fair, balanced, responsible coverage of Islam, Said noted.

Islamophobia of the Western media

Western media wield considerable influence in many Third World countries. In an extremely able survey, Daya Kishen Thussu demonstrated that the Western media 'project Islam as inimical to civilized values. The demonizing of Islam fits in well with the western geo-political interests in arms and oil. Today, after the demise of communist states, when Islam is being seen as a security threat to the West, the media in the Muslim world need to devise ways and means to reduce the dependency on western news sources'.[22]

The writer pointed out that 'with the expansion of western electronic empires, western media have instant global reach through satellite and cable technology. Western and, more specifi-

cally, Anglo-American media dominate the world's online
services, television, radio and print journalism.

'The bulk of international television news is disseminated
through western news organizations – both raw footage from TV
news agencies such as Reuters Television, Worldwide Television
News and APTV, and completed reports from satellite and cable-
based organizations such as CNN, Sky and BBC. The Voice of
America and the BBC World Service, with their various language
services, dominate the world's airwaves.

'Of the world's four biggest international news agencies –
Associated Press, United Press International, Reuters and Agence
France Presse, the first three are Anglo-American, and between
them the four disseminate nearly 80 per cent of global news.
Despite having international staff these companies promote, con-
sciously or unconsciously, a western, and more specifically, an
Anglo-American, news agenda.'

Moreover, virtually all major English-language newspapers
and news magazines in India proudly carry regular commentaries
and features from western newspapers and magazines, thanks to
syndication arrangements. Thus western news organizations wield
great influence in setting and then building a global news agenda
conforming to western interests.

Many Indian journals 'mimic' the idiom of Western media
and adopt their language, values and styles. Thussu cites a specific
instance. When P.V. Narasimha Rao visited the United States in
1994 one Indian periodical ran a 20-page cover story, 'Pan-
Islamic Fundamentalism Exporting Terror' on the so-called threat
from militant Islam that India faced.

A consultation paper produced by the Commission on British
Muslims and Islamophobia, set up by the Runnymede Trust in
1996, entitled *Islamophobia*, provides illustrative example of the
results which the media and the burden of history have produced
in British society. The Commission was headed by Prof. Gordon

Conway, Vice-Chancellor of the University of Sussex. Among its members were: Dr Zaki Badawi, Principal of the Muslim College, London, The Rt Revd Richard Chartres, Bishop of London (to December 1996), Ian Hargreaves, editor of the *New Statesman*, Dr Philip Lewis, adviser on inter-faith issues to the Bishop of Bradford, Zahida Manzoor, chair of Bradford Health Authority, Rabbi Julia Neuberger, trustee of the Runnymede Trust, Trevor Phillips, chair of the Runnymede Trust, Dr Sebastian Poulter, reader in law at the University of Southampton, Usha Prashar, civil service commissioner, Nasreen Nehman, trustee of the Runnymede Trust, Saba Risaluddin, director of the Calamus Foundation, Imam Dr Abduljalil Sajid, director of the Sussex Muslim Society, Dr Richard Stone, chair of the Jewish Council for Racial Equality, and Revd John Webber, adviser on inter-faith issues to the Bishop of Stepney.

Conway wrote in his foreword: 'If you doubt whether Islamophobia exists in Britain, I suggest you spend a week reading, as I have done, a range of national and local papers. If you look for articles which refer to Muslims or to Islam you will find prejudiced and antagonistic comments, mostly subtle but sometimes blatant and crude. Where the media lead, many will follow. British Muslims suffer discrimination in their education and in the workplace. Acts of harassment and violence against Muslims are common'.

The Consultation Paper said: 'Islamophobia is dread or hatred of Islam and of Muslims. It has existed in western countries and cultures for several centuries but in the last twenty years has become more explicit, more extreme and more dangerous. It is an ingredient of all sections of the media, and is prevalent in all sections of society'.

It listed seven features of Islamophobic discourse: '1. Muslim cultures seen as monolithic and unchanging. 2. Claims that Muslim cultures are wholly different from other cultures. 3. Islam perceived as implacably threatening. 4. Claims that Islam's adherents use their faith mainly for political or military advantage. 5. Muslim criticisms of Western cultures and societies rejected out of hand. 6. Fear of Islam mixed with racist hostility to immigration. 7. Islamophobia assumed to be natural and unproblematic'.

There are four main perceptions of 'Islam as a threat': Muslim colonization; chief threat to global peace; 'there will be wars'; and 'the hooded hordes will win'. This is what Charles Moore, editor of *The Spectator*, wrote: 'You can be British without speaking English or being Christian or being white, but nevertheless Britain is basically English-speaking, Christian and white, and if one starts to think that it might become basically Urdu-speaking and Muslim and brown, one gets frightened and angry. . . . Because of our obstinate refusal to have enough babies, Western European civilization will start to die at the point when it could have been revived with new blood. Then the hooded hordes will win, and the Koran will be taught, as Gibbon famously imagined, in the schools of Oxford'.[23]

Readers of the RSS organs *Organiser* and *Panchjanya* (Hindi) will be struck by the affinities between Islamophobes in the West and in India, very 'natural allies'.

CHAPTER 3

THE MEANINGS
OF
JIHAD AND FATWA

' The highest form of jihad is to speak the truth in the face of an unjust ruler', reads an impeccably authenticated saying of Prophet Muhammad.[1] It alone suffices to dispel the long-held, but utterly false impression, among Muslims no less than the rest, that jihad is synonymous with warfare.

The word jihad simply means 'to exert'. Ijtihad is exertion of the intellect and is a recognized source of Islamic law, Sharia. Majid Khadduri, an Iraqi jurist who won academic fame in the United States, stated that Muslim jurists 'have distinguished four different ways in which the believer may fulfill his jihad obligation: by his heart, his tongue, his hands and his sword'. Citing this dictum, Dr Roland E. Miller, an Islamist who worked as an ordained Lutheran missionary in India from 1953 to 1976, writes: 'The ordinary distinction today is between the spiritual and physical forms of striving. Spiritually, it means engaging in a battle against sin and Satan in one's own life. This is called "the greater jihad". Applied to the physical realm, the exertion means righteous warfare. This is called "the lesser jihad". A well-known Hadith reports that the Prophet Muhammad gave top precedence to the greater jihad, humanity's spiritual struggle against evil.

'Many Muslims realize that the word jihad has become a disturbing term for non-Muslims, who connect it with religious extremism and indiscriminate violence. Muslims do not look at it that way. For them the word signifies a positive religious concept which may be and frequently is misinterpreted either by Muslims themselves or by non-Muslims. A comparison will make the point clear. The term "crusade" is widely used by many people who see no problems with it and employ it innocently to describe peaceful religious gatherings. At the same time, however, when Muslims hear this word, they experience feelings of distress because it conveys to them an old message of religious violence and suffering. Precisely the same is true with the word jihad. Muslims use it in a positive sense to signify an important religious truth, while to many others it carries a message of needless religious violence.'[2]

The wars launched by the imperial Muslim dynasties – the Umayyads, the Abbasids, the Fatimids and the Ottomans – were not exercises in jihad. Still less the crimes which Muslim extremists advocate or commit in the name of Islam. Miller adds: 'Many contemporary Muslims emphasize spiritual struggle as "the bottom line" implication of jihad. They regard the rules established for the medieval period of Muslim empires as outdated and inappropriate for the needs of contemporary Muslims. . . . The so-called "Islamic Jihad" groups have no right to take this authority to themselves. In addition, their extremist methods that involve violence against the innocent have no basis in Islamic law. In the moderate view Jihad is still necessary, but it must now be directed toward two issues: the individual's struggle for piety, and society's struggle for justice'.[3]

Greater jihad, lesser jihad

In a brilliant exposition of the concept of jihad, a Beirut academic, Yusuf Ibish, wrote: 'The Greater Jihad is fighting one's animal tendencies. It is internal rather than external: striving in the path of God to overcome one's animal side. Man shares with animals certain characteristics which, if let loose, make him a very dangerous beast. To bring these passions under control, that is what Jihad means. Man has a tendency to overestimate himself – and to underestimate his spiritual potential. He has a tendency to control and exploit his environment and other human beings.

Jihad is essential against such tendencies.

'The Lesser Jihad – fighting on behalf of the community, in its defence – is a duty incumbent on a Muslim provided he is attacked. A man has the right to defend his life, his property, and he has to organize himself along these lines. Of course, one can produce incidents in history and ask whether in fact the principle of self-defence applies. It is true that Muslims have waged wars; wars of conquest, wars in the ordinary sense, often not at all related to religion or faith. But this indicates that some Muslims have not exercised the Greater Jihad.'[4]

Jihad has now become 'a pejorative codeword for random protest' against a regime in power, as Prof. Bruce B. Lawrence remarked in his stimulating work, *Shattering the Myth: Islam Beyond Violence.*[5] But, properly understood, jihad has a relevance in modern society, provided it is shorn of the connotation of violence and is informed by a moral purpose – justice for the underprivileged. 'Jihad has come to mean the advocacy of social justice in a widening circle that also includes economic participation and prosperity for Muslims' in the modern context, not for Muslims alone.[6]

This is a challenge which both Muslims and non-Muslims face today: to read the fundamentals propounded in the Quran and in the Prophet's injunctions in the context of the times and to adapt them to the conditions of modern society. For instance, Prophet Muhammad said that he is not a Muslim who eats his fill while his neighbour goes hungry. How does one adapt this 1,400-year-old injunction to modern society? It cannot mean the immediate neighbour, as in olden times. In this writer's opinion, it enjoins clearly a commitment by Muslims of India to join the struggle for the economic uplift of India's underprivileged, cutting across the religious divide. Lawrence holds that 'the future may yet belong to those who learn to wage economic jihad in [the] English [language]'.[7]

Long before the Iranian Revolution, Ayatollah Mortaza Motahhari, a cerebral cleric, wrote a small pamphlet entitled *Jihad: The Holy War of Islam and its Legitimacy in the Quran*. In his view, as Lawrence sums up, 'the only enemy to be opposed are soldiers on the battlefield, and even then only after they have been declared transgressors'.[8] Motahhari said: 'I do not think that anyone has any doubts that the holiest form of jihad and the holiest form of war is that which is fought in defence of humanity and of humanity's rights'.[9]

It must not be overlooked that Prophet Muhammad preached the message of Islam in the midst of persecution. He was compelled to emigrate to Medina to save his life. As Karen Armstrong points out, 'Islam has been dubbed the religion of the sword, a faith which has abandoned true spirituality by sanctifying violence and intolerance. It is an image that has dogged Islam in the Christian West ever since the Middle Ages, even though Christians were fighting their own holy wars in the Middle East at this time. . . . Unlike Jesus, however, Muhammad did not have the luxury of being born "when all the world was at peace". He was born into the bloodbath of seventh-century Arabia where the old values were being radically undermined and nothing adequate had yet appeared to take their place. . . . Muhammad had arrived in Medina in September 622 as a refugee who had narrowly escaped death. He would continue to be in mortal danger for the next five years, and during this time the *umma* (the community) faced the possibility of extermination. In the West we often imagine Muhammad as a warlord, brandishing his sword in order to impose Islam on a reluctant world by force of arms. The reality was quite different. Muhammad and the first Muslims were fighting for their lives and they had also undertaken a project in which violence was inevitable'.[10]

Like Miller, Armstrong demonstrates how false the popular concept of jihad is. Her exposition merits quotation: 'The Quran began to urge the Muslims of Medina to participate in a Jihad. This would involve fighting and bloodshed, but the root JHD implies more than a "holy war". It signifies a physical, moral, spiritual and intellectual effort. *There are plenty of Arabic words denoting armed combat, such as harb (war), sira's (combat), Ma'araka (battle) or qutal (killing), which the Quran could easily have used if war had been the Muslims' principal way of engaging in this effort.* Instead, it chooses a vaguer, richer word with a wide range of connotations. The jihad is not one of the five pillars of Islam. It is not the central prop of the religion, despite the common Western view. But it was and remains a duty for Muslims to commit themselves to a struggle on all fronts – moral, spiritual and political – to create a just and decent society, where the poor and vulnerable are not exploited, in the way that God had intended man to live. Fighting and warfare might sometimes be necessary, but it was only a minor part of the whole jihad or struggle. A well-known tradition (*hadith*) has Muhammad say on returning from a battle: "We return from the little jihad to the greater jihad", the more difficult and crucial effort to conquer the forces of evil in oneself and in one's own society in all the details of daily life'.[11]

A writer in the Jamaat-e-Islami's organ *Radiance Viewsweekly*, Sayed Abdullah S.M., quoted the same saying of the Prophet and proceeded to distinguish jihad from the doctrine of 'the just war' propounded in the writings of St Thomas Aquinas.[12] He acknowledged: 'There is no gainsaying the fact that Muslim rulers like their contemporaries, and in accordance with the prevailing Machiavellian statecraft, indulged in unscrupulous acts, committed atrocities and excesses. They were self-seeking rulers, power, wealth and ambition were their motives. They violated the Islamic code of conduct with impunity, for instance Mahmood of Ghazni attacked the Hindu rulers and plundered the Somnath temple. *It must be noted that he even planned to attack the Islamic Caliph of Basra.* Pandit Nehru gave a vivid account of such

Muslim rulers in his *Discovery of India* and *Glimpses of World History*, and effectively rebutted the charge that they were motivated by religious doctrine. Such rulers were Muslims by chance and not by choice'.

The Prophet's jihad

Amazingly, few have cared to consult the classic on the subject: *A Critical Exposition of the Popular 'Jihad'* by Maulvi Chiragh Ali. It was appropriately dedicated to his soulmate, a fellow rationalist and Islamic reformer, Syed Ahmad Khan.[13]

A Note explains why he embarked on the work of stupendous research: 'I here take the opportunity of removing a wrong idea of the alleged injunction of the Prophet against our countrymen, the Hindus. The Hon'ble Raja Siva Prasad, in his speech at the Legislative Council, on the 9th March, 1883, while discussing the Ilbert Bill, quoted from Amir Khusro's *Tarikh Alai* that, "Ala-ud-din Khiliji once sent for a Kazi, and asked him what was written in the Code of Muhammadan law regarding the Hindus. The Kazi answered that, the Hindus were zimmis [condemned to pay the jizya tax]; if asked silver, they ought to pay gold with deep respect and humility; and if the collector of taxes were to fling dirt in their faces, they should gladly open their mouths wide. God's order is to keep them in subjection, and the Prophet enjoins on the faithful to kill, plunder and imprison them, to make Mussulmans, or to put them to the sword, to enslave them, and confiscate their property . . . ."[14]

'These alleged injunctions, I need not say here, after what I have stated in various places of this book regarding intolerance, and compulsory conversion, are merely false imputations. There are no such injunctions of the Prophet against either zimmis [i.e. protected or guaranteed], or the Hindus.'

Chiragh Ali, a civil servant in Hyderabad State, was a close associate of Syed Ahmad Khan. Aziz Ahmad says that he 'developed some of [Syed Ahmad Khan's] ideas with consummate scholarship. But his mind was no pale reflection' of his friend. 'It is most probable that both influenced each other. Of the two, Chiragh Ali had a more scholarly knowledge of Hebrew and the Old Testament. He had, besides, at least a working knowledge of French.'[15]

Muhammad began to preach the message of Islam in 612. Before long the fierce tribe of Quraysh began persecuting him. In 615, before his own emigration to Medina in 622, a party of 11 Muslims emigrated to Ethiopia, followed the next year by another party of 100. The Quraysh sent an emissary to the Christian ruler, Negus Armuh, to obtain their surrender. The Prophet's migration to Medina (hijrah, the opening of the Muslim calendar) was treated as an act of war. Chiragh Ali takes the reader through the events that followed, culminating in Muhammad's entry into Mecca and the success of his mission in Arabia. Each battle is carefully analysed. Every single verse in the Quran on jihad is quoted and its context set out with full references in the footnotes.

Chiragh Ali does not confine his narrative to this aspect alone. Throughout his book he is at pains to distinguish between the jihad which the Prophet fought and the ones which were fought in the name of Islam by Muslim rulers: 'There was no pretence of former injuries on the part of the Moslems to make war on the Koreish. They were actually attacked by the Koreish and were several times threatened with inroads by them and their allies. So it was not until they were attacked by the enemy that they took up arms in their own defence, and sought to repel and prevent hostilities of their enemies. The defence set up for Muhammad is not equally availing of every sanguinary and revengeful tyrant. It was not only that Muhammad was wronged or attacked, but all the Moslems suffered injuries and outrages at Mecca, and when expelled therefrom, they were attacked upon, were not allowed to return to their homes, and to perform the pilgrimage there. The social and religious liberty, a natural right of every individual and nation, was denied them. A cruel or revengeful tyrant may not be justified in taking up arms in his own defence, or in seeking to redress his personal wrongs and private injuries; but the whole Moslem community at Mecca was outraged, persecuted and expelled – and the entire Muhammadan commonwealth at Medina was attacked, injured and wronged – their natural rights and privileges were disregarded – after such miseries the Moslems took up arms to protect themselves from the hostilities of their enemies and to repel force by force; and were justified by every law and justice'.[16]

The Medina verses

Muhammad faced persecution for about sixteen years, from the third year of his mission to the sixth year after the hijrah. The RSS supremo, K.S. Sudarshan, has quoted two verses from the Quran to show how Muslims have used their scripture selectively to take to the path of intolerance and bloodshed.[17] One reads: 'And fight them until persecution is no more and religion is all for Allah'.[18] That is all he quoted. It is, however, part of two connected verses which are set out below:

'38. Say to those who disbelieve, if they desist, that which is past will be forgiven them; and if they return then the example of those of old has already gone.

'39. And fight with them until there is no more persecution, and all religion is for Allah. But if they desist, then surely Allah is Seer of what they do.'

The context of these Medina verses is relevant. The Meccans had gone away from the battle of Bader in defeat, quite discomfited. The verses enjoined the Muslims not to pursue them and to desist from fighting any further, once their own persecution had ceased. Muhammad Asad's excellent commentary on the Quran explains the import of these verses: 'Both these passages stress self-defence – in the widest sense of the word – as the only justifica-tion of war'.[19]

Sudarshan quoted another verse thus: 'Then, when sacred months have passed, slay the idolators wherever ye find them, and take them (captive), and besiege them, and prepare for them each ambush. But if they repent and establish worship and pay the poor due, then leave their way free. Lo! Allah is forgiving, merciful (Sura 9: 5)'.[20] Sudarshan cites this to show how Muslims have taken to the path of intolerance and conflict.

Prof. Clinton Bennett understood the verse differently. He was once Assistant Chaplain at Westminster College, Oxford. His book, *In Search of Muhammad*,[21] is an earnest effort by a devout Christian to understand Muhammad, and places him in the ranks of others whose services Minou Reeves acknowledges in her survey of Western writings on Muhammad.

Referring to this very verse, Bennett wrote: 'This verse has indeed been so used but this is to remove the verse both from the context of what the Quran says about war (defensive, or to right a wrong) and from the context of Quranic exegesis. Scholars point out that the words "but if they repent . . . leave their way free", contained in the same verse . . . clearly indicate that the "unbe-lievers" must have initiated some type of attack against the Muslims. Indeed, the verse probably refers to the existing conflict between the Muslims and their opponents, thus giving Muslims permission to re-engage after the religious truce had ended. Arguably, the Quran is ambiguous on "whether offensive war for the faith or only defensive war" is permitted. Doner suggests that the issue is "really left to the judgement of the exegete". Afazlur Rahman Islam, however states that "Muhammad never fought against peaceful people or those who desire peace . . . only against those who continued armed resistance". Non–Muslim images of Muhammad as warlike contrast sharply with many Muslim descriptions. For example Muhammad Ali says that Muhammad had "no inclination for war", the Prophet, he says, "was peace-loving by nature". Forward agrees: "The Prophet was a reluctant warrior".'[22]

Asad's commentary supports Bennett's view. The verse 'relates to warfare *already in progress* with people who have become guilty of a breach of treaty obligations and of aggression. . . . As I have pointed out on more than one occasion, *every verse of the Quran must be read and interpreted against the background of the Quran as a whole.* The above verse, which speaks of a possible conversion to Islam on the part of "those who ascribe divinity to aught beside God" with whom the believers are at war, must, therefore, be considered in conjunction with several fundamental Quranic ordinances. One of them, "There shall be no coercion in matters of faith" (2: 256), lays down categorically that any attempt at a forcible conversion of unbelievers is prohibited – which precludes the possibility of the Muslims' demanding or expecting that a defeated enemy should embrace Islam as the price of immunity. Secondly, the Quran ordains, "Fight in God's cause against those who wage wars against you, *but do not commit aggression, for verily, God does not love aggressors*" (2: 190); and, "if they do not let you be and do not offer you peace, and do not stay their hands, seize them and slay them whenever you come upon them: and it is against these that we have clearly empowered you (to make war)" (4: 91). Thus, war is permissible *only in self-defence* (see Sura 2, verses 167 and 168), with the further proviso that "if they desist – behold, God is much-forgiving, a dispenser of grace" (2: 192), and "if they desist, then all hostility shall cease" (2: 193). Now the enemy's conversion to Islam – expressed in the words, if they repent, and take to prayer (literally "establish prayer") and render the purifying dues (zakat) – is no more than one, and by no means

the only, way of their "desisting from hostility" and the reference
to it in verses 5 and 11 of this surah certainly does not imply an
alternative of "conversion or death", as some unfriendly critics of
Islam choose to assume. Verses 4 and 6 give a further elucidation
of the attitude which the believers are enjoined to adopt towards
such of the unbelievers as are not hostile to them (in this connection, see also 60: 8–9)'.[23]

Chiragh Ali's citation of verses from the Quran yields the
same conclusion. He places another verse, often misquoted to
misrepresent jihad (2: 189), in its context: 'The verses 186, 187,
188 and 189, if read together, will show that the injunction for
fighting is only in defence. The verses are:

> 186. And fight for the cause of God against those who fight
> against you: *but commit not the injustice of attacking them first;
> verily God loveth not the unjust.*
> 187. And kill them wherever ye shall find them; and eject
> them from whatever place they have ejected you; for (fitnah)
> persecution is worse than slaughter; yet attack them not at the
> sacred Mosque, until they attack you therein, but if they
> attack you, then slay them: such is the recompense of the
> infidels:
> 188. But if they desist, then verily God is Gracious, Merciful –
> 189. And do battle against them until there be no more
> (fitnah) persecution and the only worship be that of God; *but
> if they desist, then let there be no hostility, save against wrong-doers.*'

It is not difficult to appreciate how a wholly false impression can
be created by isolating a single verse and by quoting it out of
context.

Muslim jihadists are as practised offenders as the Sudarshans.
In Islam the concept of jihad is inextricably linked to the concept
of 'oppression'. The Quran is replete with references to protec-

tion of the oppressed and to forbearance from aggression. 'But what hath come to you that ye fight not on the path of God, and for the weak among men, women and children, who say, 'O our Lord: bring us forth from this City whose inhabitants are oppressors; give us a champion from thy presence; and give us from thy presence a defender?'" (4: 75). Also, 'Permission (to fight) is given to those on whom war is made because they are oppressed. And surely Allah is also to help them' (22: 39). Nor is the unbeliever to be deprived of protection: 'If any one of those who join gods with Allah ask an asylum of thee, grant him an asylum, in order that he hear the Word of God; *then let him reach his place of safety*. This, for that they are people devoid of knowledge' (9: 6). The overriding injunction is: 'There is no compulsion in religion' (2: 256).

Having refuted Western and Indian critics of jihad, Chiragh Ali went on an offensive against Muslims whose notions of jihad were no better. The Quranic verses must be read in the proper context, he repeatedly insisted, and demonstrated how some Muslim commentaries, including the famous Hedaya, misled Muslims and non-Muslims alike: 'I will not hesitate in saying that generally the Muhammadan legists, while quoting the Koran in support of their theories, quote some dislocated portion from a verse without any heed to its context, and thus cause a great and irreparable mischief by misleading others, especially the European writers. . . . '[24]

He amplified: 'That the Koran did not allow war of aggression either when it was revealed, or in future as the early jurisconsults did infer from it, will be further shown from the opinions of the early Moslems: legists of the first and second century of the Hegira, like Ibn (son of) Omar the second Khalif, Sotian Souri, Ibn Shobormah, Ata, and Amar-bin-Dinar. All these early legists held that the fighting was not religiously incumbent (wajib), and that it was only a voluntary act, and that *only those were to be fought against who attacked the Moslems*'.[25]

Chiragh Ali found support for his views in the writings of a European scholar, Edward William Lane, who admitted: 'Misled by the decision of those doctors, and an opinion prevalent in Europe, I represented the laws of "holy war" as more severe than I found them to be according to the letter and spirit of the Kuran, when carefully examined, and according to the Hanafee code. I am indebted to Mr. Urquhart for suggesting to me the necessity of revising my former statement on the subject; and must express my conviction that *no precept is to be found in the Kuran, which, taken with the context, can justify unprovoked war*'.[26]

Jihad in our times

Reformer that he was, the battle against the jihadists of the times was only a front for Chiragh Ali's war against ignorance and conservation. 'The Koran keeps pace with the most fully and rapidly-developing civilization, if it is rationally interpreted, not as expounded by the Ulema in the Common Law Book and enforced by the sentiment of a nation. It is only the Muhammadan Common Law, with all its traditions or oral sayings of the Prophet – very few of which are genuine reports, and the supposed chimerical concurrence of the learned Moslem Doctors and mostly their analogical reasonings (called Hadees, Ijma, and Kias), passed under the name of Fiquh or Shariat – that has blended together the spiritual and the secular, and has become a barrier in some respects regarding certain social and political innovations for the higher civilization and progress of the nation. But the Koran is not responsible for this all.'[27]

Over a century later, in a speech to American religious leaders in New York, President Muhammad Khatami of Iran censured the jihadists of today whom he aptly called nihilists: 'It assumes various names, and it is tragic and unfortunate that some of those names bear a resemblance to religiosity and some proclaim spirituality . . .

'Vicious terrorists who concoct weapons out of religion are *superficial literalists* clinging to simplistic ideas. They are utterly incapable of understanding that, perhaps inadvertently, they are turning religion into the handmaiden of the most decadent ideologies. While terrorists purport to be serving the cause of religion and accuse all those who disagree with them of heresy and sacrilege, they are serving the very ideologies they condemn . . .

'The role of religious scholars has now become even more crucial, and their responsibility ever more significant. Christian thinkers in the 19th century put forward the idea that religion should be seen as a vehicle for social solidarity. Now that the world is on the edge of chaos . . . the notion of Christian solidarity should prove helpful in calling for peace and security; in the holy Koran human beings are invited to join their efforts in ta'awon, and ta'awon means solidarity, which can be translated into – co-operation to do good. We should all co-operate in the cause of doing good.'[28] President Khatami has urged 'a dialogue of civilizations' instead of a clash between them.

For a concept of jihad relevant to our times, we must turn to the labours of a Malaysian-based NGO, the Just World Trust (JUST). Dr Chandra Muzaffar, a distinguished academic and a committed activist, is its director. JUST organized a conference on the 'Images of Islam: Terrorising the Truth' at Kuala Lumpur from October 7–9, 1995. Its Report contains papers of remarkable insight and learning.[29]

The Report publishes the text of a most instructive paper by Chaiwat Satha-Anand (Qader Muheideen), President of the Social Science Association of Thailand, entitled 'The Non-violent Crescent: Eight Theses on Muslim Non-violent Actions'. Citing the relevant verses from the Quran, he asserts that 'Jihad is the command of Allah Almighty and the traditions of Prophet Muhammad that demand a perpetual self-reexamination in terms of one's potential to fight tyranny and oppression – a continual reassessment of the means for achieving peace and inculcating moral responsibility.

'The point, however, is not to dwell on the conventional wisdom of separating the concept of jihad into wars and self-purification. What is most important for contemporary Muslims is that jihad categorically places the notion of war and violence in the moral realm. . . . The perpetual inner and greater jihad will guide the conduct of lesser jihad in both its objectives and its conduct. This requirement in Islamic teaching raises the question of whether a lesser jihad can ever be practised in an age of mass warfare and nuclear weapons.'

He does not advocate passivity or submission to wrong. Far from it. In his view, 'a practising Muslim should possess the potential for disobedience, discipline, social concern and action, patience and willingness to suffer for a cause, and the idea of unity – all of which are crucial for successful nonviolent action'.

He propounds eight theses on Muslim non-violent action: '1. For Islam, the problem of violence is an integral part of the Islamic moral sphere. 2. Violence, if any, used by Muslims must be governed by rules prescribed in the Quran and Hadith. 3. If violence used cannot discriminate between combatants and non-combatants, then it is unacceptable to Islam. 4. Modern technology of destruction renders discrimination virtually impossible at present. 5. In the modern world, Muslims cannot use violence. 6. Islam teaches Muslims to fight for justice with the understanding that human lives – as all parts of God's creation – are purposive and sacred. 7. In order to be true to Islam, Muslims must utilize non-violent action as a new mode of struggle. 8. Islam itself is fertile soil for non-violence because of its potential for disobedience, strong discipline, sharing and social responsibility, perseverance and self-sacrifice, and the belief in the unity of the Muslim community and the oneness of mankind. That such theses of Muslim non-violent action are essential to peace in this world and

the true meaning of Islam is evident from the Quran: "Peace! –
Word (of salutation) from the Lord Most Merciful!" (36: 58).'[30]

Fatwa: edict or opinion?

Jihad has to be 'declared', and to lend it a colour of legality, it has
been traditionally 'declared' by the ulama (clergy) in fatwas.
Maulana Abul Kalam Azad treated those fatwas to withering
ridicule in his brilliant essay on the mystic Sarmad whom
Aurangzeb had sent to the gallows through a fatwa. Sarmad's
grave lies at the steps of the Jama Masjid in Delhi. Mulla Qavi, the
Chief Judge (qazi-ul-quzat), readily served as the Emperor's tool.

Azad recalled: 'Throughout the thirteen centuries of Islam the
pen of the jurists has been an unsheathed sword and the blood of
thousands of truthful persons stains their verdicts (fatwa). From
whichever angle you study the history of Islam, countless
examples will illustrate how whenever a ruler came to the point of
shedding blood, the pen of a mufti and the sword of a general
rendered him equal service. This was not confined to the Sufis and
nobles, for those ulama who were close to the seers of the
mysteries of truth and reality also had to suffer misfortunes from
the hands of the jurists and in the end obtained deliverance in
giving their lives'.[31]

The fatwa is *not an edict*; it is a mere legal opinion. Barbara
Metcalf pointed out, 'Fatwa in a Muslim State were traditionally
given by a court official, the mufti, for the guidance of the qazi or
judge'. The mufti is one learned in the law, fiqh. Once the British
Raj was established, fatwas 'were given directly to believers, who
welcomed them as a form of guidance in the changed circumstances of the day. They had, of course, no coercive power . . .
[but they] were of great moment to Muslims seeking to preserve
an authentic expression of their religion under alien rule'.[32]

Before long, the ulama, the maulvis and the imams, emerged

as political guides. Witness their power in Pakistan. Two of their leading parties are offshoots of the ones born in India – the Jamaat-e-Islami and Jamiatul Ulama-e-Hind which became Jamiat Ulama-e-Islam Pakistan.

The *Shorter Encyclopaedia of Islam* defines fatwa as 'a formal legal opinion given by a mufti, or canon lawyer of standing, in answer to a question submitted to him either by a judge or by a private individual'. On January 1, 2001, the High Court of Bangladesh ruled that a fatwa whereunder a divorced wife was forced to marry another person and get divorced by him in order to be lawfully remarried to her first husband, was illegal.

Justices Golam Rabbani and Majmun Ara Sultana observed: 'Fatwa means legal opinion; which means legal opinion of a lawful person or authority. The legal system in Bangladesh empowers only the courts to decide all questions relating to legal opinion on the Muslims and other laws in force. We, therefore, hold that any fatwa, including the instant one, are all unauthorized and illegal'. A mullah and five accomplices faced prosecution for the fatwa.

The Daily Star of January 3, 2001 remarked: 'This is a gigantic step forward we have taken in our society's modernizing process ... The fatwa has been the cause of many a woman's ruination ... it has been conveniently used by the clerics as an instrument of power-play in cohort with local influentials and a vehicle for assertion of bigoted religious authority over the community'.

Irresponsible fatwas, however, receive greater notice than Muslim censures of them. Ayatollah Khomeini's fatwa against Salman Rushdie in 1989 received short shrift from jurists of repute. The religious authorities of Saudi Arabia and the sheikhs of the prestigious mosque of al-Azhar in Cairo condemned the fatwa as illegal and un-Islamic. Muslim law does not permit a man to be sentenced to death without trial and has no jurisdiction outside the Islamic world. At the Islamic Conference of March 1989, forty-four out of the forty-five member states unanimously rejected the ruling. But this received only cursory attention in the British press and left many people with the misleading impression that the entire Muslim world was clamouring for Rushdie's blood.

In the wake of American air attacks on Afghanistan, the Darul Uloom of Deoband issued a fatwa proscribing the sale of American and British products. The Jamiat Ulama-e-Hind stated, on October 20, 2001, that the fatwa was issued in response to a query it had addressed to the seminary. As with the jihad, so with the fatwa. It is politics, not religion, which inspires cries of jihad and declaration of fatwas, exposing both to ridicule and Islam to misunderstanding and misrepresentation.

CHAPTER 4

THE VERY MODERN ROOTS OF ISLAMIC FUNDAMENTALISM

Fundamentalism is a malaise of the twentieth century. It has afflicted almost every major religious tradition, no matter how ancient – Hindu, Jewish, Christian and Muslim. Fundamentalism banishes reason from religion and compassion from faith. Its main traits are: revivalism, hostility towards minorities, anti-intellectualism, intolerance, arrogant insularity, intellectual bankruptcy, and moral blindness. They are reflected in a rejection of rational discourse, pluralism, free speech, democratic governance, secularism and in a recourse to violence. Not one of the fundamentalist movements has a programme of social uplift and equality or economic progress. Their decline was predictable and was, indeed, predicted.

There is no single model of fundamentalism. There is little in common between the Islamic fundamentalists of Central Asia and those in, say, Algeria. Some fundamentalists tactically contested elections; others kept out of the democratic process. The causes also varied from fear of acculturation to revolt against corruption.

Karen Armstrong asks us to 'remember that "fundamentalism" has surfaced in most religions and seems to be a world-wide response to the peculiar strain of late-twentieth century life. Radical Hindus have taken to the streets to defend the caste system and to oppose the Muslims of India; Jewish fundamentalists have made illegal settlements on the West Bank and the Gaza Strip and have vowed to drive all Arabs from their Holy Land; Jerry Falwell's Moral Majority and the new Christian Right, which saw the Soviet Union as the evil empire, achieved astonishing power in the United States during the 1980s. It is wrong, therefore, to assume that Muslim extremists are typical of their faith'.[1]

Fundamentalism is a response to the challenges of modernity which were perceived by the zealous as threats to the integrity and survival of their faith. Some of the believers met the challenge by reform and compromise; others, by rejection and retreat into revivalism. A section of the revivalists, disdaining retreat, adopted the aggressive stance of fundamentalism in thought and violence in action.

United colours of fundamentalism

Few have studied the phenomenon with such erudition and insight as Karen Armstrong, one of the foremost commentators on religious affairs in both Britain and the United States. In her study *The Battle for God* she looks at American Protestant fundamentalism, Jewish fundamentalism in Israel and Muslim fundamentalism in Egypt and Iran. The Introduction reminds the reader that fundamentalism is 'not confined to the great monotheisms. There are Buddhist, Hindu, and even Confucian fundamentalisms, which also cast aside many of the painfully acquired insights of liberal culture, which fight and kill in the name of religion and strive to bring the sacred into the realm of politics and national struggle'.[2]

The reminder is particularly necessary in India. On December 15, 2001, Prime Minister Atal Behari Vajpayee, a member of the Bharatiya Janata Party – described as a Hindu Nationalist Party by his senior colleague L.K. Advani, the Union Home Minister – attacked the religious education being given in some madrasas (Muslim religious schools).[3] Not once has he criticized, however mildly, the kind of education and training in militancy being imparted in the shakhas (branches) of the BJP's mentor, the Rashtriya Swayamsevak Sangh (RSS).[4] Taking the cue from Vajpayee's remarks, the RSS 'stepped up its campaign to shut down the madrasas and absorb the students in government-run schools'.[5] The BJP regime tries desperately to prove that fundamentalism resides among the Muslims exclusively while working overtime to implement its own fundamentalist agenda in education and other spheres of public life.

In India, Hindu fundamentalism is in the driving seat of power. In Pakistan, the Muslim fundamentalist Jamaat-e-Islami repeatedly received a drubbing at the polls. It won respectability under General Zia-ul-Haq. Benazir Bhutto entered into a partnership with the Jamiat Ulama-e-Islam Pakistan (Fazlur Rehman Group) during her second and disastrous tenure in office (1993–97).[6] Nawaz Sharif courted the Islamic fundamentalists in his own manner. The President of Pakistan, General Pervez Musharraf's historic speech on January 12, 2002, revealed a grim determination to wipe out the gains of the fundamentalists in his country, who built up street power in order to compensate for their lack of electoral support.

In India, the RSS wields street power to buttress the political clout of its political arm, the BJP. Even a fleeting glance at its fundamentalist credo reveals the menace it poses to Indian democracy. Its bible is the former RSS supremo M.S. Golwalkar's book, *A Bunch of Thoughts*. It is revivalist to the core. 'At the very outset, let it be made clear that it is not the modern thinkers who are the first in the field to think in terms of world unity and universal welfare. Long long ago, in fact, long before the so-called modern age had set in, the seers and savants of this land had delved deep into this vital question. The ideal of human unity, of a world free from all traces of conflict and misery has stirred our hearts since times immemorial.'[7]

Being a reaction to modernity, fundamentalism reared its head first in the United States, the show case of modernity. 'Of the three monotheistic religions, Islam was in fact the last to develop a fundamentalist strain, when modern culture began to take root in the Muslim world in the late 1960s and 1970s. By this date, fundamentalism was quite well established among Christians

and Jews, who had had a longer exposure to the modern experience. . . . They are all – even in the United States – highly critical
of democracy and secularism.'[8]

Scholars demur at the use of the term 'fundamentalism'.
Webster's Tenth New Collegiate Dictionary defines it as a 'movement
in 20th century Protestantism emphasizing the *literally* interpreted
Bible as fundamental to Christian life and teaching'. These literalists, in all faiths, seek to replicate the past. Which is why mainstream or liberal Christians regard the term as pejorative and
scholars shy away from its original connotations.[9] Islamic fundamentalism is 'a loose and inaccurate term that designates a number
of different, and sometimes contrasting, forms of Islamic religious
militancy'.[10] But the term has come to stay and is used because it is
the only one that encapsulates the myriad movements which share
its distinctive traits.

Some scholars prefer the word 'Islamists' to describe those
who treat Islam purely as a political ideology, shorn of the essence
of the faith. Islamism describes 'the "ideologization" of Islam at
the political level, the construction of a political ideology using
some symbols culled from the historical repertoire of Islam, to the
exclusion of others. This ideology, sometimes referred to as
"Islamic fundamentalism", is better described as Islamism: the Latin
suffix attached to the Arabic original more accurately expresses the
relationship between the pre-existing reality (in this case a religion)
and its translation into a political ideology, just as communism ide-
ologizes the reality of the commune, socialism the social, and
fascism the ancient symbol of Roman consular authority. Islamism
is not Islam. Though the lines dividing them are frequently
blurred, it is important to distinguish between them'.[11]

Shapers of Islamic fundamentalism

Two themes inspire the so-called Islamic fundamentalist – the ideal of the Islamic State and the use of jihad as a weapon for its realization. More than any others, three personalities shaped the ideology – Hasan al-Banna (1906–49), who founded the al-Ikhwan al-Muslimin, or the Muslim Brotherhood in Egypt; Sayyid Qutb (1906–66), who succeeded him as its leader on al-Banna's assassination in 1949; and Maulana Abul A'la Maududi (1903–70), who founded the Jamaat-e-Islami in Lahore on August 26, 1941.

As a young teacher, al-Banna was deeply influenced by the ideas of reformers like Muhammad Abduh (1849–1905), widely regarded as the father of Egyptian modernism; Jamal al-Din al-Afghani (1838–97), a vigorous advocate of Pan-Islamism and staunch opponent of Western colonialism, who for some time collaborated with Muhammad Abduh; and Muhammad Rashid Rida (1865–1935), a Syrian who went to Egypt to study and became a disciple of Muhammad Abduh.

It was the charismatic al-Banna who turned the ideas of these reformers into a mass movement. Armstrong relates how one evening, in March 1928, six of the local workers in Ismailiyyah came and asked him to take action: 'We know not the practical way to reach the glory of Islam and to serve the welfare of the Muslims. We are weary of this life of humiliation and restriction. So we see that the Arabs and the Muslims have no status and no dignity. They are not more than mere hirelings belonging to foreigners. We possess nothing but this blood . . . and these souls . . . and these few coins. We are unable to perceive the road to action as you perceive it, or to know the path to the service of the fatherland, the religion and the ummah as you know it'. Banna was moved by this appeal. Together, he and his visitors made an oath to be 'troops (jund) for the message of Islam'. That night the Society of Muslim Brothers was born.[12]

The Brotherhood had 2,000 branches throughout Egypt when al-Banna died in 1949. Each branch had 300,000 to

600,000 members. He had successfully mobilized Islam as a powerful revolutionary force. Sayyid Qutb joined the society in 1953 and became its leader. Al-Banna had been assassinated in 1949, reportedly by King Farouk's secret police.

Both al-Banna and Qutb wrestled with the issues that trouble the Muslim world to this day. How can Islam respond to the needs of modern times? Is the Islamic concept of state and society relevant today? Both were convinced that Islam provides a comprehensive answer, but their styles varied a lot. Though deeply religious, Qutb started out as an admirer of Western culture and its secular politics. British and French colonialism in North Africa and West Asia and Western support of Zionism added to the disillusionment he felt after a period of study in the United States. He, however, remained a moderate and aspired to give parliamentary democracy in his region an Islamic flavour. Nasser's drive for secularism and a long spell in prison in 1954 wrought a radical change in his thinking. He had been sentenced to fifteen years' hard labour and remained in prison until 1964 where he witnessed the torture and execution of Ikhwan members. Qutb was sent to the gallows in 1966 by Nasser on a charge of plotting the overthrow of his regime.

While in prison Qutb became a jihadist. His writings served as a guide to rebels. Armstrong regards him as 'the real founder of Islamic fundamentalism in the Sunni world'. To Ayatollah Ruhollah Khomeini goes the honour of its leadership in the Shiite world.

Malise Ruthven summed up the enormous impact of Qutb's writings on the entire Arab world: 'His ideas set the agenda for Islamic radicals throughout the Sunni Muslim world. Groups influenced by them included Shukri Mustafa, a former Muslim Brotherhood activist and leader of a group known as *Takfir wa Hijra* (excommunication and emigration) who followed the early Kharijis in designating grave sinners (in this case the government) as *kafirs* (infidels); Khalid Islambuli and Abdal Salam Faraj, executed for the murder of President Anwar Sadat in October 1981; and the *Hizb al-Tahrir* (Liberation Party) founded in 1952 by Sheikh Taqi al-Din al-Nabahani (1910–77), a graduate of al-Azhar, and whose writings lay down detailed prescriptions for a restored caliphate.'[13]

It is generally accepted that Maulana Abul A'la Maududi influenced both al-Banna and Qutb; though his influence was more on the latter. Maududi began his public career in 1920 when, at the age of seventeen, he became chief editor of *Taj*, an Urdu weekly. Frédéric Grare has traced his subsequent career and summed up his thinking ably in his book *Political Islam in the Indian Subcontinent*. He records: 'In response to an advertisement in the *Tarjuman al Quran*, seventy-five persons met at Islamia Park in Lahore on August 26, 1941. There Maududi delivered a speech during which he announced the main objectives of his organization. He affirmed notably: that while the other movements remained content with incorporating some parts of Islam or some objectives accepted by all Muslims, the objective of the Jamaat was to promote Islam in its totality; that the Jamaat would adopt the same system of organization as adopted by the Prophet; that ultimately the Jamaat would not restrict its activities to Indian Muslims alone but would appeal to Muslims the world over. With this the Jamaat was born'.[14]

Maududi was opposed to the Muslim League's demand for Pakistan on the ground that nationalism was against the Islamic concept of the unity of the ummah (community of the faithful). But he went over to Pakistan on its establishment and soon emerged as a supple politician, as skilled in intrigues as in polemics.

'Like any ideologist, Maududi was not developing an abstruse scholarly theory, but issuing a call to arms. He demanded a universal jihad, which he declared to be the central tenet of Islam.

No major Muslim thinker had ever made this claim before. It was an innovation required, in Maududi's eyes, by the current emergency. Jihad ('struggle') was not a holy war to convert the infidel, as Westerners believed, nor was it purely a means of self-defence, as Abduh had argued. Maududi defined jihad as a revolutionary struggle to seize power for the good of all humanity. Here again, Maududi, who developed this idea in 1939, shared the same perspective as such militant ideologies as Marxism. Just as the Prophet had fought the jahiliyyah, the ignorance and barbarism of the pre-Islamic period, so all Muslims must use all means at their disposal to resist the modern jahiliyyah of the West. The jihad could take many forms. Some people would write articles, others make speeches, but in the last resort, they must be prepared for armed struggle.

'Never before had jihad figured so centrally in official Islamic discourse. The militancy of Maududi's vision was almost without precedent, but the situation had become more desperate since Abduh and Banna had tried to reform Islam and help it to absorb the modern Western ethos peacefully. Some Muslims were now prepared for war. One of the people most profoundly affected by Maududi's work was Sayyid Qutb. . . .

'Yet Qutb went much further than Maududi, who had only seen the non-Muslim world as jahili. By the 1960s, Qutb was convinced that the so-called Muslim world was also riddled with the evil values and cruelty of jahiliyyah. Even though a ruler such as Nasser outwardly professed Islam, his words and action proved that he had in fact apostatized. Muslims were duty-bound to overthrow such a government. He now looked back to the life and career of the Prophet to create an ideology that would mobilize a dedicated vanguard in a jihad to turn back the tide of secularism and force its society to return to the values of Islam.'[15]

Fundamentalism deserves severest censures for the intolerance it fosters and the violence it advocates. But it is given to few to go beyond censure and try to understand why men of learning and moral sensitivity came to embrace so sterile and destructive an ideology. Qutb was a tragic figure. 'He respected reason and science but did not see them as the sole guides of truth. During his long years in prison, at the same time as he evolved his new fundamentalist ideology, he worked on a monumental commentary on the Koran, which showed his spiritual awareness of the ineffable and the unseen. No matter how rational the human intellect became, he wrote, it was constantly swimming in "the sea of the unknown". All philosophical and scientific developments certainly constituted progress of a sort, but they were simply glimpses of permanent cosmic laws, as superficial as the waves "in a vast ocean; they do not change the currents, being regulated by constant natural factors". Where modern rationalism concentrated on the mundane, Qutb still cultivated the traditional discipline of looking through the earthly reality, which saw worldly events as reflecting more or less perfectly eternal, archetypal realities, was crucial to his thought. Its apparent absence in the United States had disturbed him. When Qutb gazed at modern secular culture, like other fundamentalists he saw a hell, a place utterly drained of sacred and moral significance, which filled him with horror.'[16]

None of this inhibits Karen Armstrong from this justly deserved severe censure of the man: 'But by making jihad central to the Muslim vision, Qutb had in fact distorted the Prophet's life. The traditional biographies make it clear that even though the first ummah had to fight in order to survive, Muhammad did not achieve victory by the sword but by a creative and ingenious policy of non-violence. The Koran condemns all warfare as abhorrent, and permits only a war of self-defence. The Koran is adamantly opposed to the use of force in religious matters. Its vision is inclusive, it recognizes the validity of all rightly guided religion, and praises all the great prophets of the past. The last time Muhammad preached to the community before his death, he urged Muslims to use their religion to reach out to others in understanding, since all human beings were brothers: "O men: behold we have created you all out of a male and a female, and have made you into nations and tribes so that you may know one another." Qutb's vision of exclusion and separation goes against this accepting tolerance. The Koran categorically and with great emphasis insisted that "There shall be no coercion in matters of faith." Qutb qualified this: there could only be toleration after the political victory of Islam and the establishment of a true Muslim state'.[17]

No less devastating is her censure of Maududi, who was a far more worldly man than Qutb, and on the same ground, namely, distortion of the message of Islam. 'Maududi argued that jihad was the central tenet of Islam. This was an innovation. Nobody had ever claimed before that jihad was equivalent to the five Pillars of Islam, but Maududi felt that the innovation was justified by the present emergency. The stress and fear of cultural and religious annihilation had led to the development of a more extreme and potentially violent distortion of the faith.'[18]

In Pakistan a Court of Inquiry, comprising Justice M. Munir as President and Justice M.R. Kayani as Member, enquired into the disturbances in 1953 in Punjab. It exonerated Maududi of personal responsibility but trenchantly criticized the ideology he and his associates were espousing. The Court heard many a cleric, including Maududi: 'The ulama (clergy) were divided in their opinions when they were asked to cite some precedent of an Islamic State in Muslim history. Thus, though Hafiz Kifayat Husain, the Shia divine, held out as his ideal the form of Government during the Holy Prophet's time, Maulana Daud Ghaznavi also included in his precedent the days of the Islamic Republic of Umar bin Abdul Aziz, Salahud-din Ayyubi of Damascus, Sultan Mahmud of Ghazni, Muhammad Tughlq and Aurangzeb and the present regime in Saudi Arabia. Most of them, however, relied on the form of Government during the Islamic Republic from 632 to 661 A.D., a period of less than thirty years, though some of them also added the very short period of Umar bin Abdul Aziz. Maulana Abdul Haamid Badayuni stated that the details of the ideal State would be worked out by the Ulama'.[19]

They differed not only on the powers of the modern legislature but also on the need for legislation. Sayyid Qutb held that a Muslim 'cannot practice his Islam except in a Muslim milieu where Islam is sovereign. Otherwise he is misguided in thinking that he is able to realize Islam while he is a lost or persecuted individual in jahili (barbaric) society'.[20]

What is an 'Islamic' state?

Nothing betrays the paucity of thought of the so-called fundamentalists more than the answers they give to the fundamental question: Why an Islamic State? Maulana Abul A'la Maududi's answer is a typical one: 'The Quran not only lays down principles of morality and ethics, but also gives guidance in the political, social and economic fields. It prescribes punishment for certain crimes and enunciates principles of monetary and fiscal policy. These cannot be translated into practice unless there is a State to enforce them. And herein lies the necessity of an Islamic State'.[21]

Shorn of verbiage, it comes to no more than that an Islamic State is necessary in order to enforce the Islamic law of crimes. Is, then, a Muslim who lives in a secular State, or any State which is not an 'Islamic' State, any the less Muslim for that? The suggestion that the ambience of an Islamic State would encourage Muslims to practice the tenets of Islam drew from the Munir Report withering scorn: 'Our politicians should understand that if Divine Commands cannot make or keep a man a Musalman, their statutes will not'.[22]

Nor are the fundamentalists interested in defining the status of non-Muslims in an Islamic State in terms which even enlightened Muslims can understand. Their effect on non-Muslims can be easily imagined. Any one who reads recent literature on Islam produced by the so-called fundamentalists will be struck by their total lack of interest in the subject. It reflects far more than bankruptcy of thought. It betrays a complete absence of moral purpose, and an obsession with political power, for which Islam is being cynically exploited.

For, if they were at all concerned with defining the relevance of Islam to the Muslim of today, they could have hardly overlooked the millions who live in India, the republics of the former Soviet Union, China and, indeed, the entire world outside the Muslim countries. Has Islam no message for them, for their rights in, and their duties towards, their countries and their fellow-citizens? There assuredly is a problem of redefinition here; for their situation is different from any they have known in the past.

Rather than draw farfetched conclusions about institutional forms from ethical precepts, would it not be more to the point to apply the precepts to the conditions of today? For instance, Prophet Muhammad said: 'He is not a faithful who eats his fill while his neighbour remains hungry by his side'. He, surely, did not enjoin concern for a Muslim neighbour alone. Are these forceful words of no relevance for the Muslim as he looks around him and sees poverty and degradation in his country? Is its plight of no moment to him because the majority of its citizens are non-Muslims? One would think that this is a clear injunction for commitment to social and economic equality in the country, cutting across its religious divide.

Nor are the apologists agreed on whether the consensus is to be of the people as a whole or only of the learned. In a collection of lectures delivered in Iraq in 1970, entitled 'Islamic Government', Khomeini asserted that 'since Islamic government is a government of law, it is the religious expert (faqih) and no one else who should occupy himself with the affairs of government'.

However, the fact of the matter is, as was boldly stated by A.K. Brohi in a series of articles in *Dawn* in 1952: 'Having regard to the accepted notion of what constitutional law is, it is not possible to derive from the text of the Quran any clear statement as to the actual content of the constitution of any State'. But the most devastating refutation comes from Ibn Khaldun, acknowledged as one of the greatest historians of all time: 'Some wrongly assume the imamate to be the pillars of faith. It is one of the general (public) interests. The people are delegated to take care of it. If it were one of the pillars of the faith, it would be something like prayer, and Muhammad would have appointed a representative, exactly as he appointed Abu Bakr to represent him at prayer'.[23]

Maududi's debating tactics verge on the pathetic. To give an example, Muhammad Asad translates a verse in the Quran (22:41) thus: 'God is most powerful, almighty, (well aware of) those who, (even) if we firmly establish them on earth, remain constant in prayer, and give in charity, and enjoin the doing of what is right and forbid the doing of what is wrong; but with God rests the final outcome of all events'.[24] This is how Maududi interprets it: 'This verse states clearly the aims, objects and duties of an Islamic State. Unlike a Secular State, its duty is not merely to maintain internal order, to defend the frontiers and to work for the material prosperity of the country. Rather, its first and foremost obligation is to establish the systems of salat (prayer) and zakat, to propagate and establish those things which are considered to be "virtues" by God and His Messenger, and to eradicate those things which have been declared to be "vice" by them. In other words, no state can be called Islamic if it does not fulfill this fundamental objective of an Islamic State. Thus a state which does not take interest in establishing virtue and eradicating vice and in which adultery, drinking, gambling, obscene literature, indecent films, vulgar songs, immoral display of beauty, promiscuous mingling of men and women, co-education, etc., flourish without let or hindrance, cannot be called an Islamic State. An Islamic Constitution must declare the above mentioned objective as the primary duty of the State'.[25] The Quranic verse is however translated thus: '(Muslims are) those who, if we give them power in the land, establish the system of Salat (worship) and Zakat (poor-due) and enjoin virtue and forbid evil'.

In truth, there is no such thing as an *Islamic* State; indeed, there simply *cannot* be one. For Islam shapes the personality of man, and of society through him. It does not provide for the institutions of government, for these vary with time, whereas the fundamentals of the faith are valid for all time. Virtue cannot be ordained by the State. Yet, it is this mirage of the Islamic State which Islamic fundamentalists have sought all these years.

In Pakistan, advocates of the Islamic State unearthed an old treatise entitled *Ahkam al-Sultaniyyah* (Ordinances of Government) written by al-Mawardi (991–1031). He was the first writer on political theory in the history of Islam. The flaws in his analyses received devastating treatment in a monograph by Qamaruddin Khan. The writer pointed out that 'the Quran has not defined any clear principle of state. The meaning and idea of the constitution, the clear conception of sovereignty, the principle of franchise, the detailed conception of human rights, and the regulations of state organization are not given anywhere'.[26]

After the first four Caliphs who succeeded Prophet Muhammad, 'the idea of the democratic Caliphate passed into a monarchical system without any ideological conflict. . . . It was this theory of nomination that cut at the very root of democratic ideals in Islamic polity. It has been persistently resorted to by every Muslim ruler after the days of the Pious Caliphate, to perpetuate dynastic and despotic rule among the Muslim peoples. Thus, apparently the structure of the Caliphate was maintained by the Umayyads, the Abbasids, the Fatimids, and the Turks but the spirit of Islamic democracy was buried in the coffin of Ali, the last of the Pious Caliphs'.

Al-Mawardi sought to justify the changes in the character of the Caliphate brought about by monarchical rule. He left a baleful legacy. It 'completely changed the concept of Muslim polity in the centuries that followed. And the change that occurred was simply un-Islamic, undemocratic, and vicious'. It was supported by twisting the texts of the Quran and 'fabricating numerous traditions along with ingeniously prepared chain of transmitters'.[27]

Qamaruddin Khan proceeded to argue that the citizen had a right to rebel if the ruler deviated from the law and trampled on his rights. He concluded by tearing apart the theories built on the treatise by al-Mawardi. 'Even the recent upsurge of revivalism in the Muslim world has broken no ground. It goes on repeating the propositions of al-Mawardi blindly. It has utterly failed to grasp the driving democratic force of ancient Islam. It has not realized in the least that the mission of the Holy Prophet Muhammad is for all climes and for all times. The Quran and the Sunnah, therefore, must be reinterpreted so as to solve the major problems of man in modern society. But to refuse to recognize these problems and to wish that the present-day world may direct its affairs according to dogmas and traditions which have no reality in fact and experience, is to expect too much of human forbearance.'

Maududi had no hesitation in describing his model as a 'theodemocracy'. Khomeini championed rule by the clergy – *Vilayat Faqih* (Vice-regency of Islamic jurists) – in his book, *The Theologians' Guardianship*.

The failure of fundamentalism

One of the Arab world's most distinguished journalists, Muhammad Heikal, a close friend of President Nasser, has explained why the credo of fundamentalism appealed to the Arab masses despite its narrowness: 'A lack of moral leadership made millions of Arab minds receptive to the call of the Iranian revolution across the Gulf, reminding them vaguely of values embedded in their faith. The disaffected masses rediscovered their religious heritage with an enthusiasm which took everyone by surprise. It was not that Islam had been neglected during the decade of illusions – more that its commandments had ceased to be taken seriously. Islam was about to renew itself, resuming its role as an anchor for millions who were spiritually adrift. It was time for a return to fundamentals'.[28]

It was this deep sense of betrayal which hurt more than military defeat by the Zionists, who were supported by the United States and Britain. Arabs *knew* how utterly corrupt their rulers were: 'The Zionist Organization and the British Government continued to bribe influential Arabs. President Roosevelt told Chaim Weizmann that, in his opinion, the Arabs could be bought; Weizmann responded that he had heard something to that effect. In the minutes of their conversation the Arabic word *baksheesh* appears. The Jewish Agency's biggest client seems to have been Prince Abdallah of Transjordan'.[29]

Disenchanted, the people turned to their faith for succour. 'The masses were looking for new certainties, but what they found were old ones, reminders that Islam is in essence a revolt of the poor. The Prophet Muhammad depended on fighters from the Mustadafeen, the exploited weak and poor, to help him overcome the hostility of the wealthy. Mecca was ruled by the Mustaqbireen, meaning the self-inflated rich and powerful, whose commercial interests were threatened by the Koran, the divine message conveyed through Muhammad. His teachings, compiled to form the Sunna, retained their relevance through the centuries, and were a constant solace for the oppressed. The effect of the Iranian revolution was to rekindle the original energy of these texts through fresh interpretations.'[30]

Unfortunately, it was not a creative interpretation which they heard but a singularly restrictive one; from none other than Maududi. Heikal perceptively notes: 'By 1980 it [the Arab world] was beginning to feel the influence of Muslims from Pakistan and India, where Islam had acquired a different flavour. Asian Muslims tended to take the Koran literally, while Arabs were more inclined to interpret it. *Reading the texts in their own language enabled Arabs to set it in historical context, keeping in mind observations by religious authorities, but Asians were less able to look beyond it* – partly because other works had not been translated into their languages, but more importantly because the Arabic language was the tongue of Islam. Deprived of linguistic context the Koran inevitably takes on a slightly different character, forcing non-Arab readers to rely more on the texts than on the way the ideas are expressed'.[31]

Maududi's work was translated into Arabic in the late 1950s and early sixties, and had a considerable impact on a new generation of Muslim Brotherhood members and other Arabs. His ideas were also taken up by Sayyid Qutb.

'Islam had migrated from the Arab world to the east, *then returned home with an Indian accent* and a strong militant message which made the masses in Cairo, Beirut and elsewhere more receptive when the Islamic revolution exploded in Tehran. The poverty belts around the big cities became a natural breeding ground for a militant, anti-elitist, anti-Western view of Islam. Amid chaos and confusion and loss of identity among people displaced from their home villages, Islam was not just a refuge but a battle cry.'[32]

A contemporary analysis of the phenomenon of re-Islamization, by Detlev H. Khalid, bears recalling today.[33] Of Moroccan descent, Khalid was born in Berlin and was educated in Germany and Spain. He wrote: 'Fundamentalist Islam in the last quarter of the 20th century has been graced with a promising constellation: Libya and Saudi Arabia provide the financial capital; Egypt and Pakistan supply the ideological know-how'.

What is of compelling interest is his analysis of fundamentalism *as a last ditch attempt to stop the tide of reform*. 'Up to a few years ago there was a feeling among young academics that *a breakthrough was near at hand, that it was only a matter of time before the great revolution in Muslim religious thought would erupt. There can be little doubt that once the process is set into full motion there will be as much turmoil as during the European enlightenment*.

'The fundamentalists do, of course, know what is in the offing. Much of their sudden haste to enforce the canon law (shari'a) is due to the realization that if they do not act swiftly and stem the tide in the last minute, their chances will be swept away. Thus there is a level on which re-Islamization does not testify to the strength of the formalist zealots, *but rather to their weakness. At a moment when the rock of traditionalism was in the final stage of erosion it was shored up by the petro-dollar, but it is doubtful if this underpinning will last*. For many Muslim intellectuals, leftists and liberals alike, the resurgence of Saudi-backed fundamentalism has come as a devastating blow at a time when they were preparing to assume responsibility for the cultural destiny of their society. Faced with the financial might of the Wahhabi octopus they have not yet regained enough morale to line up for a counteroffensive. For the time being, there is but little intellectual guerilla warfare.'[34]

Therein lay the seeds of the failure of fundamentalism. Mark Huband, Cairo correspondent for the *Financial Times*, noted the early signs of its retreat. 'The late 1990s have been dominated by the shattering of unity within the Islamist movements, which began the decade with the conviction that it was only a matter of time before their demands would be met. The bloody first days of 1998 saw calls by the Algerian Islamic Salvation Front for a negotiated settlement of the Algerian crisis, while the rival Armed Islamic Group (GIA) continued to slaughter; demands by the imprisoned leaders of the Egyptian al-Gama'a al-Islamiyya for a resumption of the cease-fire they had called for in 1997, while its radical militants rejected calls for moderation; softening of the Islamist policies, at least in foreign affairs, of the Sudanese government, while hard-liners continued the onslaught against southern rebels.

'The disarray within the most active Islamist movements during 1997–98 has now, in 1999, evolved further, resulting in what appear to be significant steps toward a reassessment of their future strategies. On 25 March 1999, the jailed leaders of Egypt's al-Gama'a al-Islamiyya, in concert with its leaders in exile, declared a further ceasefire in their conflict with the government.'[35]

The classic on this subject is, beyond a doubt, the distinguished French scholar and acknowledged authority Olivier Roy's work, *The Failure of Political Islam*. He points out that 'first of all Islamization will mean the destruction of the social space between the state and the family. The Islamic society to which neo-fundamentalism refers never existed. The Islam that the FIS (Islamic Salvation Front) is proposing is (unfortunately) not a return to Muslim civilization: this civilization had its golden age long ago, before its internal decline and the arrival of colonialism, but the FIS, like all neofundamentalist organizations, rejects the very notion of Muslim civilization, which had room for music, philosophy, poetry and, as we have seen . . . a certain secularity. *What the Islamists advocate is not the return of an incomparably rich classical age, but the establishment of an empty stage on which the believer strives to realize with each gesture the ethical model of the Prophet.* The only place for conviviality here is the family, which is also, but only for men, the only place of pleasure. . . .

'What will imposition of the sharia mean? Hypocrisy. For, as the true ideologues of Islamism have always said, from Sayyid Qutb to Maududi and Khomeini, imposition of the sharia makes sense only if the society is already Islamic and man finally virtuous.

If not, everything is just casuistics, appearance and ruse, the use of which may be perfectly legal (hile shar'i: "legal ruse", the kind that allows the believer to get around a shariatic interdiction without falling into a state of sin).'[36]

In an excellent paper which Roy read at a seminar in New Delhi in November 2001, a copy of which he kindly furnished to the writer, Roy analysed the tragic course of events in Talibanized Afghanistan ('Bin Laden – An Apocalyptic Sect Severed from Political Islam'). *Bin Laden was not an heir of the fundamentalists.* He was on a murderous frolic of his own. 'There is a fundamental difference that marks a break between the activities of Bin Laden's networks and previous Islamic radicalism: no political strategy whatsoever underlies these activities. Attacks carried out by Palestinians always aim to attract attention to their cause and raise the costs of occupying the territories and colonies. The attacks of 1983 and 1984 in Lebanon, followed by the taking of hostages, were an attempt to force Western troops to withdraw from Lebanon and to oblige France to cut off its support for Iraq. The attacks of 1995 and 1996 in France, whoever the actual perpetrators were, had the goal of persuading France to stay out of Algerian affairs. The attacks against the American troops in Saudi Arabia sought to force their retreat.

'But what was the objective of the September 11 attacks? The destruction of capitalism and modern-day Babylon? No strategy underlies these attacks because they have no attainable goal. The paradoxical result is that no negotiations are possible, even if they were desirable, because there are no demands. What is at stake is the symbolic dramatization of the apocalypse. In contrast to previous attacks, moreover, no shadow of a state looms behind the destruction of the World Trade Center. The Taliban are merely accused of harbouring Bin Laden, not of sponsoring the attacks. The break with important Islamic movements (Hezbollah, Iran, Muslim Brotherhood, Islamic Salvation Front [FIS], and Turkish ex-Refah) is evident in the fact that such groups condemn the attacks. Those who support Bin Laden (Pakistani religious movements, the *Hizb ul Tahrir* based in London) belong, in contrast, to a different current than the important Islamist parties.'

In this context, one is at a loss to know how to characterize the utterances of the Shahi (Royal) Imam of Jama Masjid in Delhi, Syed Ahmed Bukhari. He said on November 9, 2001: 'I support the jihads that Muslims have unleashed in the US and have no sympathy for those dead in September 11 attacks. In fact no Muslim should stop and rest till the US is completely destroyed. The US will then understand what Muslim nations have gone through over the years because of the atrocities meted out to them by the US. I hope the US is erased from the face of this earth by our Muslim fighters'.

He also attacked the President of Pakistan in his speech: 'Pervez Musharraf has bowed his head in front of the US which is beneath any Muslim. Muslims should understand that the US can cut off their heads but cannot make us bow to their tyranny. The target of America and its allies is not Afghanistan or Taliban but Islam which is proved by the fact that US only sees terrorism in Muslim countries. I hope Musharraf is thrown out of his powers and his government falls'.[37] This is not even fundamentalism. It is rank political opportunism shorn of all pretence to ideology, and devoid of any religious commitment or humanity. 'I have no fear in saying that I don't feel an inch of sympathy for those who died in the September 11 attacks. America should see its mothers crying, America should see its children suffering. Only then would they realize what it means to be attacked, like Palestine has been attacked or like Iraq has been attacked,' he said in an interview. Bukhari disclosed: 'I spoke to the Prime Minister and asked him why we are supporting the US. *He assured me that India would never supply air space and re-fuelling facilities to US war-planes. And the next day I called a press conference'*.[38]

The disclosure is interesting. In March 1977, Vajpayee had shared the platform at a public meeting in Delhi with his inter-locutor's father, the then Shahi Imam, Syed Abdullah Bukhari. On November 21, 1979, during the campaign for election to the Lok Sabha, Indira Gandhi wrote a letter to him giving assurances of redress of specific Muslim grievances. Encouraged by politi-cians of all hues, men such as these hold themselves forth as mediators between the State and a hapless, aggrieved minority, exploiting the concerns of both and stoking the embers of bigotry to keep their enterprise going.

Maulana Nomani of the Jamiat-ul-Ulema-e-Hind told the correspondent: 'The appointment of an Imam is not by succes-sion, and only muftis can issue fatwas or any religious order. Only the Amir of an Islamic state has the authority of calling for jihad'. The Central Advisory Council of the Jamaat-e-Islami Hind adopted a resolution on November 9, 2001 which was in striking contrast: 'In the eyes of the Central Advisory Council (CAC) of Jamaat-e-Islami Hind, terrorism is an outright oppressive act. This session of the CAC considers it condemnable whether it is committed by an individual or a group or a State, and whosoever is its target. Some people having immoderate sentiments associate terrorism with religion while religion strictly opposes it. As for Islam, killing an innocent person is tantamount to killing all human beings, and saving the life of a person is saving the entire human folk.

'The September 11 attacks on the two cities of America are highly condemnable. The CAC extends its sympathy with the families of the victims of these attacks, and considers it very necessary to get it thoroughly investigated so that those who are really responsible for these attacks may be duly punished. To this session of CAC it is very wrong and unjust that an action is taken against an individual or individuals without any proof. Hence the American attack on Afghanistan is indeed an oppressive and terroristic act which is condemnable from every angle as innocent persons are being killed everyday and no one knows how long this aggression will continue.'[39]

The Organization of the Islamic Conference (OIC) took a similar position but refrained from criticizing the United States' military action in Afghanistan. The Ninth Extraordinary Session of Foreign Ministers of the OIC issued, at Qatar on October 10, 2001, a communiqué which said: 'The conference strongly condemned the brutal terror acts that befell the United States, caused huge losses in human lives from various nationalities and wreaked the tremendous destruction and damage in New York and Washington. . . . The Conference stressed that such shameful terror acts are opposed to the tolerant divine message of Islam which spurns aggression, calls for peace, coexistence, tolerance and respect among people, highly prizes the dignity of human life and prohibits killing of the innocent. It further rejected any attempts alleging the existence of any connection or relation between the Islamic faith and terrorist acts. . . . The Conference expressed its concern over the possible consequences of the fight against terrorism including the death of innocent civilians in Afghanistan, and underlined the necessity of ensuring the territorial integrity of Afghanistan and its Islamic identity. It rejected the targeting of any Islamic or Arab State under the pretext of fighting terrorism'.

Roy's paper noted three trends that have now come to the fore: 'On the one hand, pressure from Islamists, combined with the desire on the part of regimes already in power to endow themselves with religious legitimacy, led almost everywhere to the conservative re-Islamization of these societies, primarily in regards to rights and morality. In fact, this re-Islamization has now slipped from the control not only of Islamist movements but also of reigning governments, insofar as it has facilitated the emergence of new figures who cannot be situated within the perspective of the distribution of state power (public figures and preachers, but also terrorists). Re-Islamization is carried out outside any prospect of obtaining power, producing what might be called post-Islamism.

'On the other hand, Islamist movements are currently taken up by the logic of integration into the national political scene. Having become "Islamonationalists", they are confronted with the necessity of reformulating their ideology so as to obtain an equal footing in the political game, provided it is not already a closed contest. Finally, the consequence of these two phenomena is that terrorism and Islamic radicalism have been pushed to the margins of the Muslim world, both geographically (to Afghanistan and New Jersey) and sociologically (the Armed Islamic group [AIG] and the perpetrators of the attacks against the WTC), in the form of Sunni fundamentalism which is ideologically conservative but politically radical.

'This dissociation between national Islamism and peripheral radicalism provides the regimes in power with more room to manoeuvre, but it by no means encourages them to become more open politically. Thus Islamism always provides a single ideology of popular mobilization and protest, which feeds on the deficit of democracy, as well as the increasing hostility to the United States in Muslim public opinion. Almost all major Islamist movements have abandoned the terrain of political violence to become more nationalist than Islamist, although their domestic political policies remain extremely conservative.'

Bin Laden's Al Qaeda had no stakes in real social concerns. 'He brings the possibility of vengeance to the frustrated, but embodies neither hope nor alternative. . . . There is no specific political project, no brighter future. . . . It is more implicated in problems of existence and identity than in a logic of class or conflicts of interest.'

That is true of all fundamentalists, Muslim as much as others. Osama Bin Laden's discourse is, however, even less intelligible and is coarse. In an interview with Hamid Mir, editor of the Urdu daily *Ausaf*, he said: 'America and its allies are massacring us in Palestine, Chechnya, Kashmir and Iraq. The Muslims have the right to attack America in reprisal. The Shariat says that Muslims should not live in the land of the infidel for long. The September 11 attacks were not targeted at women and children. The real targets were America's icons of military and economic power. . . . The American people should remember that they pay taxes to their Government, they elect their President, their Government manufactures arms and gives them to Israel and Israel uses them to massacre Palestinians. The American Congress endorses all Government measures and this proves that the whole of America is responsible for the atrocities perpetrated against Muslims.

'I ask the American people to force their Government to give up anti-Muslim policies. . . . I say that if we don't get security, the Americans too will not get security'.[40]

This is nothing but lumpenization of fundamentalism, be it in reprisal for a recent wrong or an imagined one centuries ago, as happened in the demolition of the Babri mosque in Ayodhya in 1992. On more substantive issues, as the Lebanese scholar Asad Abu Khalil pointed out, in the writings of fundamentalists on economics, agriculture, industrialization and the like, what one finds for the most part are vague formulae.[41]

Re-imagining Islam

In the wake of the attack on the World Trade Center on September 11, 2001, American reaction was divided. There were those who resented any suggestion that the horrendous crime was perpetrated by men who sought vengeance for American policies in Palestine and elsewhere in West Asia. Others, while refusing for a moment to belittle the monstrosity of the crime, nonetheless felt that the United States had long been *callously* insensitive to Arab and Muslim sentiment. Exploitation of Islam as a political tool was not confined to the fundamentalists. The United States used it in the so-called 'jihad' against the Soviet Union in Afghanistan, in concert with its allies, Saudi Arabia and Pakistan.

The Taliban and Osama Bin Laden have been destroyed at great cost. But the passions, fears and hatreds on which they thrived, linger, and are unlikely to diminish. Popular alienation persists and it is not unlikely that, far from being subdued by recent events, including demonstration, of America's military might, it will deepen further still. Fundamentalism brooks no compromise and lies discredited, anyway. It is exposed thoroughly for its political blunders, moral wrongs and intellectual errors. If malaise is an apt word to describe it, its eradication will not be possible unless the underlying causes are addressed. Like the forms which fundamentalism assumed in various faiths and regions, the causes also varied. In the Muslim world, prime among the causes were denial of democratic rights, political oppression, and the sordid and enduring alliance between Western power and corrupt despots. The West, especially the United States has a lot to answer for. It has yet to demonstrate a willingness to learn from the tragedy of the WTC.

The Muslim political class and the intelligentsia are not free from blame, however. They yielded valuable space to fundamentalism, and at times collaborated with it. Intellectual and cultural stagnation amidst economic despair and social inequality posed moral and intellectual challenges which few cared to meet. The void was filled by forces of destruction who spoke in the name of Islam but were impervious to its commandments of tolerance and compassion. In the name of Islam, they took to the path of violence.

Nothing but daring creativity in thinking, and a resolute determination to recapture the essence of Islam and relate it to the conditions of today, can lift Muslims from the morass in which they find themselves.

CHAPTER 5

HUMAN RIGHTS IN THE ISLAMIC TRADITION

'Those Eastern thinkers of the ninth century laid down, on the basis of their theology, the principle of the Rights of Man, in those very terms, comprehending the rights of individual liberty, and of inviolability of person and property; described the supreme power in Islam, or Califate, as based on a contract, implying conditions of capacity and performance, and subject to cancellation if the conditions under the contract were not fulfilled; elaborated a Law of War of which the humane, chivalrous prescriptions would have put to the blush certain belligerents in the Great War; expounded a doctrine of toleration of non-Moslem creeds so liberal that our West had to wait a thousand years before seeing equivalent principles adopted. Such a height and scope of conceptions may well have sufficed to inspire silent submission in any minds not endowed with constructive genius to an equal degree; but events moreover occurred that seem to have exerted the influence of a crushing and decisive factor.'[1]

Democracy and Islam

What were those factors which deflected Muslims from following the fundamentals of Islam, a faith which enjoined respect for human rights and defined a theology of liberation? The so-called fundamentalists, who profess to speak in the name of Islam, are the very ones who show scant respect for human rights; especially the prime human right – the right to life.

Islamic thought flowered long after monarchical rule overtook the democratic Caliphate of the first four Caliphs who succeeded Prophet Muhammad after his death on June 8, 632. The poet-philosopher, Muhammad Iqbal, attributes the stagnation that gripped the Muslim world to the closing of the gates of ijtihad (reason). The rulers began to exploit religion for political ends. Jurists conformed rather than speak the truth to power.

As one recalls the texts of the early years of Islam one is struck by the violation of the fundamentals of the faith by the Muslims of today; not least, by the professional fundamentalists. In his celebrated oration at Mina in 632, Prophet Muhammad said: 'O people verily your Lord is one and your father is one. All of you belong to Adam and Adam is (made) of earth. Behold, there is no superiority for an Arab over a non-Arab and for a non-Arab over an Arab; nor for a red-coloured over a black-coloured and for a black-skinned except in piety. Verily the noblest among you is he who is the most pious'.[2]

As news of his death spread, there were those who refused to accept that the Prophet could die. Abu Bakr, who was elected to succeed him, delivered then one of the most memorable utterances in the history of Islam: 'O ye people, if any one worships Muhammad, Muhammad is dead; but if anyone worships God, He is alive and dies not'. The Prophet's biographer, Prof. W. Montgomery Watt, made the perfect comment on this episode: 'This was the quality of the faith produced by companionship with Muhammad'.[3] Abu Bakr recited the Quranic verse (3: 144): 'Muhammad is only a messenger, and the messengers before him have passed away. If he dies or is killed, will you turn on your heels?'

As the first Caliph, Abu Bakr delivered a speech which is as seminally important as his remark on the Prophet's death. He said: 'I have been given authority over you but I am not the best of you. If I do well, help me, and if I do ill, then put me right. Truth consists in loyalty and falsehood in treachery. The weak among you shall be strong in my eyes until I secure his right if God wills; and the strong among you shall be weak in my eyes until I wrest the right from him. If a people refrain from fighting in the way of God, God will smite them with disgrace. Wickedness is never widespread in a people but God brings calamity upon them all. Obey me as long as I obey God and His apostle, and if I disobey them you owe me no obedience'.[4]

This was nothing but a prescription for democratic governance under the rule of law to which even the Caliph was subject. The people's right to reject him was recognized. How many Muslim rulers of today or of the past, would speak in this idiom?

Abu Bakr, however, only followed the injunctions of the Quran. It extolled those 'who (conduct) their affairs by mutual consultation' (42: 38). In his *Tafheem-al-Quran*, Maulana Maududi comments at length on this verse. He asserts that it prescribes five principles: (*a*) the public has a right to free expressions of views; (*b*) he who is entrusted with public office should be appointed with the consent of the public, freely given; (*c*) those who advise the authorities should command the confidence of the community, and persons who attain these positions by pressure or deceit cannot command such confidence; (*d*) those who advise will render the advice in consonance with their knowledge, faith and conscience and should have full freedom to do so as otherwise the advice given will not amount to shura but to treachery; and (*e*) the advice given by the consensus of Ahl-e-Shura or which is supported by the majority of them, should be accepted since the meaning of the verse is not just to consult but to run the affairs (of the community) with mutual consultations – within, of course, the limits prescribed by religion.[5]

The Prophet himself was respected as a messenger of God. He did not claim infallibility as a mortal, nor uniqueness; still less superiority over the earlier Prophets. The Quran is explicit on these points. 'And for every nation there is a messenger' (10: 47). Further, 'We make no difference between any of His messengers' (2: 285). Some are mentioned in the Quran – Abraham, Ishmael, Isaac, Jacob, Moses and Jesus. 'We do not make any distinction between any of them' (2: 136). But this does not exhaust the number of Messengers sent by God, the Quran clearly says. The concept of 'the People of the Book' must reckon with this verse of the Quran as well: 'And (We sent) messengers we have mentioned to thee before and messengers we have not mentioned to thee' (4: 164).

The Quranic concept of human rights flows logically from the fundamentals of the faith it propounds. It envisions a *pluralist* society based on religious tolerance. 'There is no compulsion in religion' (2: 256).

Finally, 'it is not righteousness that you turn your face towards the East and the West, but righteous is the one who believes in Allah and the Last Day and the angels and the Book and the prophets, and gives away wealth out of love for Him to the near of kin and the orphans and the needy and the wayfarer and to those who ask and to set slaves free and keeps up prayer and pays the poor-rate; and the performers of their promise when they make a promise and the patient in distress and affliction and in the time of conflict. These are they who are truthful; and those who keep their duty' (2: 177).

The question of non-Muslims

The question must squarely be faced. If the ummah be the community of believers, what is its relationship with non-Muslims? The record of actual practice reveals both tolerance and intolerance towards the non-Muslims, dhimmis as they were called. They paid a tax, jizya, in return for protection and were exempt from military service. 'Under Islamic law, dhimmis enjoyed the rights to life, property, religious belief and practice, movement, marriage and the right to bring up their children according to their respective faiths . . . moreover, dhimmis enjoyed a substantial degree of autonomy or self-government which enabled members of each religious community to manage their own affairs and to settle their personal and other disputes in accordance with the rules and traditions of their respective faiths. If they were dissatisfied with their own communal justice they had the right to seek justice and settlement of disputes in Islamic courts.'[6]

The reader will notice that the Universal Islamic Declaration of Human Rights (see Appendix 1) does not list among the rights of minorities (article X) *the right to share in the governance of the State*. This is utterly unacceptable in modern times. An erudite Kashmiri scholar, Dr Sheikh Showkat Hussain, holds that 'Islam does not prohibit the participation of non-Muslims in such legislation (which conforms to Islam). Umar ibn al-Khattab (the second Caliph) sought the advice of non-Muslim experts while devising procedures for the collection of revenue and the settlement of lands in Iraq and Egypt. When Umar came to know about Binomin, a learned leader of Copts in Egypt, he asked Amr ibn al-As, the Governor of Egypt, to consult him regarding various affairs of administration'.[7]

Muhammad Talat Ghunaymi boldly charted a new course in his work, *The Muslim Conception of International Law and the Western Approach*, which Sheikh Showkat Hussain cites. Ghunaymi departs from the classical legal theory, which 'regards common creed and spiritual ideal as the delimitation of the extension of the state (and) could not comprehend the idea of nationality in its modern sense, that is to say a bond between man and a defined territory. Scholars of this view plead for a change in the classical view, as the Islamic state nowadays has become a political entity of defined territorial sovereignty'.[8]

Ghunaymi writes: 'Nowadays the Islamic state is no more a community. It has become a political entity of defined territorial sovereignty. Rulings relevant to the legal status of non-Muslims residing in the Islamic state should adapt with the present organization. Therefore, a dhimmi could generally acquire the nationality of the Islamic state in which he resides with full rights of citizenship'.[9]

Showkat Hussain's dissent bears quotation for it is based on a fundamental flaw that vitiates most Muslim writings; namely, rejection of ijtihad and, with it, a refusal to adapt the fundamentals to the conditions of today. He writes: 'It is submitted here that the states towards which reference has been made by Ghunaymi are not Islamic but national states. The basis of nationality in these states is the same as that of contemporary non-Muslim states. Non-Muslim subjects of these states have automatically acquired the nationality of these states. But this does not change the position of non-Muslim subjects in the light of the Islamic Sharia. The Sharia being based on unamendable divine revelation, cannot change along with the change of its so-called followers. There is no question of change in it even if the whole of the Muslim world deviates from it'.[10]

The sharia (Islamic) law does not bar non-Muslims from participation in the governance of the State, either. It does not provide for an Islamic State at all, as we have seen. On the other hand, the Quran lays great emphasis on the twin values of equality and justice. It is not Muslims, but mankind, which the Quran addresses when it proclaims: 'O mankind, surely We have created you from a male and a female, and made you tribes and families that you may know each other. Surely the noblest of you with Allah is the most dutiful of you' (49: 13).

In his monograph *Human Rights in Islam*, Abul A'la Maududi records: 'A woman belonging to a high and noble family was arrested in connection with a theft. The case was brought to the Prophet and it was recommended that she be spared punishment. The Prophet replied: "The nations that lived before you were destroyed by God because they punished the common man for their offences and let their dignitaries go unpunished for their crimes: I swear by Him (God) who holds my life in His hand that even if Fatima, the daughter of Muhammad, had committed this crime, then I would have amputated her hand"'.[11]

On amputation of the hand, Maududi writes: 'There are some people who take a few provisions of the Islamic Penal Code out of their context and jeer at them. But they do not realize that those provisions are to be viewed with the background of the whole Islamic system of life covering the economic, social, political and educational spheres of activity. If all these departments are not working, then those isolated provisions of our Penal Code can certainly work on miracles. For example, we all know that Islam imposes the penalty of amputating the hand for the commitment of theft. But this injunction is meant to be promulgated in a full fledged Islamic society wherein the wealthy pay zakat to the state and the state provides for the basic necessities of the needy and the destitute; wherein every township is enjoined to play host to visitors at all its own expense for a minimum period of three days; wherein all citizens are provided with equal privileges and opportunities to seek economic livelihood; wherein monopolistic tendencies are discouraged; wherein people are God-fearing. . . . In other words, it is not meant for the present-day society where you cannot get a single penny without having to pay interest . . . and where the political system serves only to prop up injustice, class-privileges and distressing economic disparities'.[12]

It did not occur to him, nor does it to his followers today, that his reasoning à propos a verse of the Quran was an exercise of ijtihad. *He read the verse in the context of the times.* This very exercise he rejects for other verses of abiding relevance and force, such as this: 'O you who believe! Be resolute in the doing of justice, as witnesses to God, even though it be against your own selves, your parents, or your kith and kin, whether it concern men rich or poor, for God is nearer to both. Do not follow your own whims lest you swerve. And if you do distort justice or decline to do it, truly, God is well-acquainted with all that you do' (4: 135). And this: 'O you who believe, be upright for Allah, bearers of witness with justice, and let not hatred of a people incite you not to act equitably. Be just; that is nearer to observance of duty' (5: 8).

The draftsmen of the *Universal Islamic Declaration of Human Rights* (Appendix I) have provided against each Article copious references to the Quran and the traditions of the Prophet (hadith). For example, the Quran enjoins respect for privacy: 'Ye who believe: Do not enter homes other than your own till you obtain permission and greet their inmates' (24: 27).

In an excellent essay on *Islam and Human Rights*, a distinguished lawyer, the late V.A. Syed Muhammad, spelt out from the texts rights to equality; to life, liberty and security of person; freedom of religion, thought and expression; freedom of movement; right to education, etc. Particularly noteworthy are these sayings by Prophet Muhammad which he quotes citing full references: 'The worst form of class prejudice is to support one's community even in tyranny', and 'He who knowingly lends support to tyranny is outside the pale of Islam'.[13]

The concept of liberation from oppression is very sharply defined in Islam.

To the scholar Asghar Ali Engineer goes the credit for drawing from the Quran a coherent theology of liberation.[14] The Quran approves of the oppressed avenging themselves: 'And vindicate themselves after they have been oppressed' (26: 227; 27: 5). Engineer writes: 'The medieval theologians emphasized giving of alms but a liberation theologian in a modern industrial society would interpret it to mean creation of a socialistic structure with emphasis on equal distribution of all available resources'.[15]

Islam sanctions distributive justice. Engineer emphasizes, however, the sharp difference between the faith as it is enunciated in the Quran, and the perversion that is fundamentalism: 'It is needless to point out that liberation theology is opposed to the fundamentalist movement as it seeks to re-emphasize traditional issues and seeks to give a new lease of life to traditional theology without concerning itself with the problems of the modern world, economic exploitation, social injustices and anti-imperialist struggles to liberate the Third World countries from the clutches of the imperialist forces'.[16]

CHAPTER 6

IJTIHAD (REASON) AND THE CHALLENGE OF MODERNITY

' ... the Musalman of today lives in the past and yearns for the return of the glory that was Islam. He finds himself standing on the crossroads, wrapped in the mantle of the past and with the dead weight of centuries on his back, frustrated and bewildered and hesitant to turn one corner or the other. The freshness and the simplicity of the faith, which gave determination to his mind and spring to his muscle is now denied to him. He has neither the means nor the ability to conquer and there are no countries to conquer. Little does he understand that the forces, which are pitted against him, are entirely different from those against which early Islam had to fight, and that on the clues given by his own ancestors, human mind has achieved results which he cannot understand. He therefore finds himself in a state of helplessness, waiting for some one to come and help him out of this morass of uncertainty and confusion. And he will go on waiting like this without anything happening. Nothing but a bold reorientation of Islam to separate the vital from the lifeless can preserve it as a World Idea and convert the Musalman into a citizen of the present and the future world from the archaic incongruity that he is today.'[1]

The Munir Report only restated the task. Muslims have long been debating on how it is to be accomplished; how to bring about an 'Orientation of Islam to separate the vital from the lifeless'. It can be done only by using reason to understand revelation. The Quran itself set a very high value on knowledge. Prophet Muhammad himself is ordered to pray: 'O Lord: increase my knowledge' (20: 114). He, in turn, asked his followers to seek knowledge even if it be from distant China.

Return to the text

There is now, as the grand Mufti of Marseille, Soheib Bencheikh, puts it, a 'flagrant anachronism separating religious thought and Muslims' real life experience . . . there must be a return to the text, and a re-reading with new intelligence, and the culture and concerns of the man of today'.[2]

If, for instance, the prescribed punishment for theft – amputation of the arm – should be limited to the ideal conditions of an Islamic State which has banished want, as Maulana Maududi argued, the exercise can surely be extended further. But was he reading the text correctly? It was said by a Judge of the United States Supreme Court that the worst way to read the two-hundred-year-old Constitution was to read it literally. Ancient scriptures deserve greater understanding. There are those who would read the text as implying no more than putting the offender out of action by imprisonment. 'Cutting off the arm' would mean no worse than 'cutting off the tongue' of the slanderer. He must be silenced, not maimed. This is true of all sacred texts.

There are Quranic verses of relevance specifically to the times; others are of universal application. There are traditions of the Prophet, collected long after his death, some of which are widely acknowledged to be zaif (infirm); others are accorded credence and acceptability. At the time of al-Bukhari, the foremost and most highly respected among the compilers of authentic hadith, there were already thousands of false accounts in circulation. That was less than two centuries after the death of the Prophet. Al-Bukhari was a man of saintly character, and a perfectionist, who did his best to sift fact from fiction.

Now, centuries later, Islam in practice bears the aspect of ossification in rituals, taboos and bans; the dross accumulated over centuries of intellectual stagnation. In a series of three articles published between January and March 1999 in *Dawn*, the late

Eqbal Ahmad analysed what he called the roots of the religious right and came down very harshly on the mutilations of Islam by absolutists whose obsession with regulating personal behaviour promoted 'an Islamic order reduced to a penal code, stripped of its humanism, aesthetics, intellectual quests, and spiritual devotion'. This 'entails an absolute assertion of one, generally decontextualized, aspect of religion and a total disregard of another. The phenomenon distorts religion, debases tradition, and twists the political process wherever it unfolds'. It is impossible 'to recognize the Islamic religion, society, culture, history or politics as lived and experienced by Muslims through the ages'.

The poet Ghalib's scathing retort to Maulvi Hamza Khan, who advised him to give up drinking, was most apt. In a letter to his friend and the Maulvi's pupil, Alauddin Ahmed Khan Alai, dated July 28, 1862, Ghalib wrote: 'To make a maulvi by teaching the baniyas [shopkeepers] and brats of Dariba [a Delhi locality] and to wallow in the problems [in religious observances] of menstruation and post-natal bleeding is one thing and to study the works of the mystics and take into one's heart the essential truth of God's reality and His expression in all things is another. . . . My belief in God's oneness is untainted, and my faith is perfect. My tongue repeats "There is no God but God," and my heart believes "Nothing exists but God, and God alone works manifest in all things." All prophets were to be honoured, and submission to each in his own time was the duty of man. With Muhammad (peace be upon him) prophethood came to an end'.[3]

Rationalism in Islam

Now that fundamentalism is discredited, are we about to witness resumption of the trend which it arrested? A 'breakthrough' and 'the great revolution in Muslim religious thought' which Detlev H. Khalid perceived before the eruption of fundamentalism?

In the Indo-Pak subcontinent there were some signs of this breakthrough even before that. There was a glimmer of hope in the nineteenth century thanks to the exertions of two outstanding personalities. One was Jamal ad-Din al-Afghani (1838–97), a staunch opponent of Western colonialism, who, though a Pan-Islamist, was a rationalist, espoused Indian Nationalism and admired Hindu thought.[4] Born and educated in Iran and then in British India, he was a teacher and tireless political activist who travelled widely from Egypt to India, and in Europe. The Egyptian reformer Muhammad Abduh (1849–1905) was his protégé.

The other towering personality was Syed Ahmad Khan (1817–98), who is better known as the founder of the Anglo-Muhammadan Oriental College which became, in 1920, the Aligarh Muslim University. This fact, and his political support for British rule, beclouded his vastly more seminal role as a great teacher and rationalist who blazed a new trail. Both Maulana Abul Kalam Azad and Muhammad Iqbal were profoundly influenced by him.

But it became a fashion to belittle him because of his politics. Jawaharlal Nehru's appreciation was fair and balanced. Syed Ahmad Khan, he wrote, 'was an ardent reformer and he wanted to reconcile modern scientific thought with Islam. This was to be done, of course, not by attacking any basic belief, but by a rationalistic interpretation of scripture. He pointed out the basic similarities between Islam and Christianity. He attacked purdah (the seclusion of women) among the Moslems. He was opposed to any allegiance to the Turkish Khalifat. Above all, he was anxious to push a new type of education. The beginning of the national movement frightened him, for he thought that any opposition to the British authorities would deprive him of their help in his educational programme. That help appeared to him to be essential, and so he tried to tone down anti-British sentiments among the Moslems and to turn them away from the National Congress which was taking shape then. One of the declared objects of the Aligarh College he founded was "to make the Musalmans of India worthy and useful subjects of the British crown". He was not opposed to the National Congress because he considered it predominantly a Hindu organization; he opposed it because he thought it was politically too aggressive (though it was mild enough in those days), and he wanted British help and cooperation.

'He tried to show that Moslems as a whole had not rebelled during the Mutiny and that many had remained loyal to the British power. He was in no way anti-Hindu or communally separatist. Repeatedly he emphasized that religious differences should have no political or national significance. "Do you not inhabit the same land?" he said. "Remember that the words Hindu and Muhammadan are only meant for religious distinction; otherwise all persons, whether Hindu or Muhammadan, even the Christians who reside in this country, are all in this particular respect belonging to one and the same nation".'[5]

Al-Afghani deplored the decline of the questioning, reflective spirit in Muslims. 'The first Muslims had no science, but thanks to the Islamic religion, a philosophic spirit arose among them, and owing to that philosophic spirit they began to discuss the general affairs of the world and human necessities . . . the first defect appearing in any nation that is headed toward decline is in the philosophic spirit. After that deficiencies spread into the other sciences, arts, and associations.'[6]

He went on to attack the ulama (clergy) for their hostility to modern science. 'How very strange it is that the Muslims study those sciences that are ascribed to Aristotle with the greatest delight, as if Aristotle were one of the pillars of the Muslims. However, if the discussion relates to Galileo, Newton, and Kepler, they consider them infidels. The father and mother of science is proof, and proof is neither Aristotle nor Galileo. The truth is where there is proof, and those who forbid science and knowledge in the belief that they are safeguarding the Islamic religion are really the enemies of that religion. The Islamic religion is the closest of religions to science and knowledge and there is no incompatibility between science and knowledge and the foundation of the Islamic faith.'[7]

Al-Afghani was unsparing in his criticism. 'Why do you not raise your eyes from those defective books and why do you not cast your glance on this wide world? Why do you not employ your reflection and thought on events and their causes without the veils of those works? Why do you always utilize those exalted minds on trifling problems? . . .

'Yet you spend no thought on this question of great importance, incumbent on every intelligent man, which is: What is the cause of the poverty, indigence, helplessness, and distress of the Muslims, and is there a cure for this important phenomenon and great misfortune or not?'[8]

Precisely the same question can be asked of the maulvis of today in the Indo-Pak subcontinent. But, as Keddie remarked, Al-Afghani would not flinch from 'insincere rhetoric' in his polemics with Syed Ahmad Khan. 'It would in fact have been difficult for Afghani to present a doctrinal argument, for his own ideas on religious reform, including greater rationalism, a return to the purer Islam of the early days, and a reopening of the door of interpretation, were very close to those of Ahmad Khan.'[9]

Except that Syed Ahmad Khan was vastly more scholarly and more rigorous in his analyses. So was his colleague, Maulvi Chiragh Ali, author of the classic on jihad and an earlier work on reform under Muslim rule.[10] Chiragh Ali wrote: 'The Muhammadan Common Law is by no means divine or super-human. It mostly consists of uncertain traditions, Arabian usages and customs, some frivolous and fortuitous analogical deductions from the Koran, and a multitudinous array of casuistical sophistry of the canonical legists. It has not been held sacred or unchangeable by enlightened Muhammadans of any Moslem country and in any age since its compilation in the fourth century of the Hejira. All the Mujtahids, Ahl Hadis, and other non-Mokallids had no regard for the four schools of Muhammadan religious jurisprudence, or the Common Law'.[11]

Syed Ahmad Khan questioned the four schools of Islamic jurisprudence (fiqh), and an uncritical reliance on hadith, which, he said led to the closing of the gates of ijtihad (reason).

Iqbal: the poet–philosopher

Iqbal's poetry held the masses in thrall, to the neglect of his contribution as a philosopher. The lectures which he delivered at Chennai, Hyderabad and Aligarh, published in book form, created a stir.[12] Lecture VI on 'The Principle of Movement in the Structure of Islam' is of great relevance even now. He asked: 'What then is the principle of movement in the structure of Islam? This is known as "Ijtihad". The word literally means to exert. In the terminology of Islamic law it means to exert with a view to form an independent judgment on a legal question. The idea, I believe, has its origin in a well-known verse of the Quran – "And to those who exert, We show our path"'.

To the question whether Islamic law was capable of evolution, Iqbal answered in an emphatic affirmative: 'I have no doubt that a deeper study of the enormous legal literature of Islam is sure to rid the modern critic of the superficial opinion that the Law of Islam is stationary and incapable of development. Unfortunately, the conservative Muslim public of this country is not yet quite ready for a critical discussion of "Fiqh" (jurisprudence)'.[13]

Iqbal was well aware of the opposition he would face from the ulama. 'I know the Ulema of Islam claim finality for the popular schools of Muhammadan Law, though they never found

it possible to deny the theoretical possibility of a complete Ijtihad.
. . . Did the founders of our schools ever claim finality for their
reasonings and interpretations? Never. *The claim of the present generation of Muslim liberals to reinterpret the foundational legal principles, in
the light of their own experience and the altered conditions of modern life,
is, in my opinion, perfectly justified.* The teaching of the Quran that
life is a process of progressive creation necessitates that each generation, guided but unhampered by the work of its predecessors,
should be permitted to solve its own problems.'[14]

What Iqbal said in 1930 is no less true now, seventy years
later. 'In view of the intense conservatism of the Muslims of India,
Indian judges cannot but stick to what are called standard works.
The result is that while the peoples are moving the law remains
stationary.'

In Iqbal's view we must distinguish traditions of a purely legal
import from those which are of a non-legal character. With regard
to the former, there arises a very important question as to how far
they embody the pre-Islamic usages of Arabia which were in some
cases left intact, and in others modified, by the Prophet. 'It is
difficult to make this discovery, for our early writers do not always
refer to pre-Islamic usages. Nor is it possible to discover that the
usages, left intact by express or tacit approval of the prophet, were
intended to be universal in their application.' He concluded that
'the closing of the door of Ijtihad is pure fiction suggested partly
by the crystallization of legal thought in Islam, and partly by that
intellectual laziness which, especially in the period of spiritual
decay, turns great thinkers into idols. If some of the later doctors
have upheld this fiction, modern Islam is not bound by this
voluntary surrender of intellectual independence'.

Iqbal himself had to face the wrath of the mullahs, as is clear
from his letter to Akbar Shah Mujibabadi: 'You are right. The
influence of the professional Maulvis had greatly decreased owing
to Sir Syed Ahmad Khan's movement. But the Khilafat

Committee, for the sake of political fatwas, had restored their influence among Indian Muslims. This was a very big mistake (the effect of) which has, probably, not yet been realized by anyone. I have had an experience of this recently. I had written an English essay on Ijtihad, which was read in a meeting here and, God willing, will be published, but some people called me Kafir. We shall talk at length about this affair, when you come to Lahore. In these days, particularly in India, one must move with very great circumspection'.[15]

Islam and politics

Fazlur Rahman, one of the most erudite and insightful scholars on Islam, had to bear the full brunt of the mullahs' opposition when he was Director of the Institute of Islamic Research in Karachi from 1962–68. He migrated to the United States, became Professor in Islamic Studies at the University of Chicago and won renown. 'The aim of the Quran is man, and his behaviour, not God', he wrote, rather provocatively. He further wrote: 'By contrast, the Muslim attitude to knowledge in the later medieval centuries is so negative that if one puts it beside the Quran one cannot help being appalled. According to this attitude, higher knowledge and faith are mutually dysfunctional and increase at each other's expense'. While neo-revivalism or neo-fundamentalism was one obstacle, another was the relationship between religion and politics and 'the pitiable subjugation' of religion to politics. In his view, 'The first essential step to relieve the vicious circle just mentioned is, for the Muslim, to distinguish clearly between normative Islam and historical Islam. Unless effective and sustained efforts are made in this direction, there is no way visible for the creation of the kind of Islamic mind I have been speaking of just now. No amount of mechanical juxtaposition of old and new subjects and disciplines can produce this kind of mind. If the spark for the modernization of old Islamic learning and for the Islamization of the new is to arise, then the original thrust of Islam – of the Quran and Muhammad – must be clearly resurrected so that the conformities and deformities of historical Islam may be clearly resurrected so that the conformities and deformities of historical Islam may be clearly judged by it.'[16]

Shabbir Akhtar belongs to the same tradition. His book, *A Faith for All Seasons*, has received little notice in India or Pakistan. His principal aim was 'to counsel Muslims to be reflective, to be intellectually honest enough to face frankly and conscientiously the tribunal of secular reason and to do so within faithful parameters. . . . My attempt at reverent skepticism in these pages is in the service of rediscovering the old Islam, not of inventing a new heresy'.[17]

The fundamentalists never tire of declaiming that in Islam, religion and politics are not separate. That is very true. But they subordinate and pervert the teachings of Islam to suit their politics instead of infusing in politics the ethical imperatives of the faith.

Islam, doubtless, is not a religion of individualistic piety but of man in society. Congregational prayer is regarded as more meritorious than prayer in solitude. Islam has a vision of economic equality, social justice, individual freedom, liberation of the oppressed and of equality of men and women. Its fundamentals do not prescribe the rules of statehood. They do ordain righteous conduct in society. These have to be adapted to meet the needs of the times.

None put it better than the former President of Iran, Ali Akbar Hashmi Rafsanjani, in a Friday sermon: 'The important point there is that the Islam which developed 1,400 years ago on the Arabian peninsula – in a settlement where the people were fundamentally nomads – was a legal code specific to that society. And even that code was promulgated slowly over a period of seven or eight years. Now the legal code which was executed in those days for that particular nation, aspires to become the code for a world in which humanity has plunged the depths of the earth . . .

'The Islam which was revealed some 1,400 years ago for the limited society of that time, now desires to become the fulcrum of (modern) social administration and (our) nation wants to use this fulcrum (as a weapon), to wage war on the entire imperialist world, testing its mettle by those means. Unique circumstances have arisen during the course of time. How can Islam (without adaptation) cover all these contingencies?'[18] His successor, President Muhammad Khatami, has called for a 'dialogue among civilizations'.

A theology of liberation

The last word on the role of Islam in politics must belong to Maulana Abul Kalam Azad, a devout Muslim and eloquent advocate of Islam's liberation theology, who fought British rule in India and steadfastly worked for national unity. Gandhi characterized his historic statement in a Calcutta court on January 24, 1922 as an oration deserving of penal servitude for life. Azad, for his part, told the court that no punishment it would award him could be equal to his 'crime', for he stood for open, if non-violent, rebellion against British rule. It was a religious duty.

'I am a Muslim and by virtue of being one, this has become my religious duty. Islam never accepts as valid a sovereignty which is personal, or is constituted of a bureaucracy, or a handful of paid executives. Islam constitutes a perfected system of freedom and democracy. It has been revealed to recover for the human race the liberty which has been snatched away from it. Monarchs, foreign domination, selfish religious pontiffs, and power brokers, all had misappropriated this liberty of man. They had been fondly nursing the belief that power and possession spell the highest right. The moment Islam appeared it proclaimed the highest right is not might but right itself. No one, except God, has got the right to make serfs and slaves of God's creatures. All men are equal and their fundamental rights are on a par. Only he is greater than others whose deeds are the most righteous of all.

'Sovereignty as defined by the Prophet of Islam and the Khalifas was a perfected concept of democratic equality, and it could only take shape with the whole nation's will, unity, suffrage and election. This is why the sovereign or a president of a republic is like a designated Khalifa. Khilafat literally means nothing more nor less than representation, so that the authority a Khalifa possesses consists in his representative role, and he possesses no power beyond this representative authority.

'Islam defines it as a duty of Muslims to refuse to acknowledge the moral justification, even of an Islamic government, if full play is not granted in it to the will and franchise of the nation. It is, then, obvious what ruling Islam would give to a foreign bureaucracy. If today there was to be established in India an Islamic government, but if the system of that government was based on personal monarchy or upon bureaucratic oligarchy, then to protest against the existence of such a government would still be my primary duty as a Muslim. I would still call the government oppressive and demand its replacement.

'I confess that this original concept of Islamic sovereignty could not be maintained because of the selfishness and personal ambition of the later Muslim sovereigns. The magnificence of the emperors of Ancient Rome and of the Shahs of Persia had attracted the Muslim sovereigns to the dubious glory of great monarchical empires. They began to prefer the majestic figures of Kaiser or Khosroe to the simple dignity of the original Khalifas, clad often times in old tattered robes. No period of the dynasties and sovereignties of Islam has, however, failed to produce some true Muslim martyrs, who have made public declarations against the tyrannies and transgressions of such monarchies, and, joyfully and triumphantly, suffered all miseries and hardships which were inflicted upon them in the thorny path of duty.

'But how would this national duty be performed? Islam has indicated three different standards under three different conditions: "If any one of you sees an evil, it is necessary that you should correct it with your own hands. If you do not have the power to do it personally you should proclaim it, and if you feel that you have not the power to denounce it, you should consider it evil in your heart at least. But this last degree is the weakest stage of religion" (a saying of Prophet Muhammad). In India we do not have the capacity to correct the evils of the government with our own hands. We have, therefore, adopted the second measure, i.e., we denounce its evils.

'The Holy Prophet of Islam has preached the following doctrine to the Muslims: "That man is blessed with the best of deaths who proclaims truth in face of a tyrannical administration and is slaughtered as punishment of this deed." The Holy Quran defines the greatest attribute of the true Muslim as "Not fearing any being except God, and whatever he considers to be truth, he recks [sic] not any authority in the public proclamation of such truth." . . . In the early Islamic days Muslims were truthful to such an extent that an old woman could in an open court, dare say to the Khalifa of the time, "If you fail to do justice, your hair would be pulled out." And instead of instituting a case against her he would thank God that such outspoken tongues were present in the nation.'

Maulana Azad concluded, 'Mr. Magistrate, I will not take any more time of the Court now. It is an interesting and instructive chapter of History which both of us are engaged in writing. The dock has fallen to our lot and to yours the magisterial chair. I admit that this chair is as necessary for this work as this dock. Come, let us finish our role in this memorable drama. The historian is eagerly awaiting, and the future is looking forward to us. Allow us to occupy this dock repeatedly and continuously, and, you may also go on writing judgements again and again. For some more time this work will continue, until the gates of another Court are flung open. This will be the Court of the Law of God. Time will act as its judge and pass the judgment. And that verdict will be final in all respects'.[19]

That was the hour of liberation theology in its best form; a true jihad against alien rule fought by non-violent means along with compatriots. A jihad is yet to be fought out against ignorance, economic deprivation, social injustice, constitutional abuse and political wrongs. In this battle, the Muslim must not only accept, but seek the association of, all, irrespective of their faith. Above all, the Muslim must wage the Greater Jihad, the Jihad-e-Akbar, within himself and in his own society. For, as the Quran says: 'Verily never will God change the condition of a people until they change it themselves' (13: 11).

CHAPTER 7

EPILOGUE:

TIME FOR THE GREATER JIHAD

Peter Hain, Minister for Europe in the Blair government, is one of Britain's most progressive ministers, with a fine record as a campaigner for civil rights and against racism. His academic credentials (Master of Philosophy) are as impressive. So are the books he has written. Lawyers of a conservative bent of mind should read his book, *Political Trials in Britain*.[1] His remarks on Muslim immigrants to Britain as 'isolationist' therefore came as a great surprise. They should prod serious reflection. The remarks were made on May 12, 2002, in interviews with *The Guardian* and *The Sunday Times*, and with the BBC.

To quote *The Sunday Times* report by Nicholas Rufford: 'Speaking in the aftermath of the murder of Pim Fortuyn, the populist Dutch politician who defended his anti-immigration policies by claiming Muslims were regressive and illiberal, Hain said problems arising from religious differences *were more dangerous* than problems of racial differences.

'"Islam is now a much bigger factor than racial tension and we are going to need to resolve that together, not by targeting Muslims as Fortuyn was doing but sending a clear message that British Muslims are welcome here and enrich our culture, *but also that they must be part of our culture*," said Hain. "*Muslim immigrants can be very isolationist in their own behaviour and their own customs*. That, in the end is going to create real difficulties and is likely to be ripe for exploitation by extremists, whether it is followers of bin Laden on one hand or racists on the other. It takes two to *integrate*, and we need to work with the Muslim community."'[2]

The Guardian's report read: 'Calling for a wider and more honest debate about asylum and immigration, Mr. Hain says: "We

need an honest dialogue about the minority of isolationists, fundamentalists and fanatics who open the door to exploitation and
who provide fertile ground for al-Qaida extremists." Muslims are
welcome but Muslim immigrants could be very isolationist and
need to integrate more, he argues. Speaking on Breakfast with
Frost, Mr. Hain added: "We need to work much harder to
integrate Muslims in particular with the rest of society. We very
much welcome the contribution that the Muslim community
makes to British culture. They enrich our culture. They are
welcome here. But there is a tendency amongst a minority to
isolate themselves and that leaves them vulnerable to either
exploitation by Osama bin Laden-type extremists and fanatics on
the one hand, or targeting by racists and Nazis on the other. And
that is where we need to work together to confront this
problem."

'His remarks brought an angry response from the Liberal
Democrat home affairs spokesman Simon Hughes. Speaking at a
rally against racism in Trafalgar Square, Mr. Hughes said:
"Identifying Muslims as the group most guilty of separatism in the
UK, as the Minister for Europe has done, is simplistic and
dangerous. *There are many national, racial and faith communities where
lack of good English and different religious traditions keep them away from
too much of mainstream British culture and participation.*"[3] The point
was well taken. The trait is common to all immigrant groups.

The Guardian's editorial the next day, May 13, entitled 'Peter
Hain Mis-hits: Separatism is not just an Islamic issue' was most
encouraging. It said: 'Where Mr Hain is wrong in today's
interview is in identifying separatism and fundamentalism as
purely an Islamic problem. There are fundamentalists in all
religions, who rightly make liberals uncomfortable. Similarly, the
Muslim community is not the only immigrant group who have
turned in on themselves. To suggest this is confined to Muslims is
damaging and wrong. We do need a grown-up debate about inte-

gration and the causes, such as white discrimination, for the growth of separatism. Evidence to the Bradford inquiry suggested the Asian community, which *arrived intent on integration, now wanted separatism*. The Ouseley report on Bradford painted a grim picture of a city retreating behind ethnic lines, with highly segregated housing and schools. Last year's race riots in the three northern towns – and the fear and distrust subsequently documented – is evidence enough of the need for better integration. The sooner debate starts the better. Remember, *integration does not mean assimilation'*. One would have thought that Hain was aware of these realities.

The last point, so tellingly made, is relevant to all plural societies – especially to India in the wake of Prime Minister Atal Behari Vajpayee's remarks at Goa, on April 12, 2002. He said: 'Wherever there are Muslims they do not want to live with others. Instead of living peacefully they want to preach and propagate their religion by creating fear and terror in the minds of others'.[4] It helped little that, as he later admitted to the speaker of the Lok Sabha, he had inserted the word 'such' before Muslims in the (sanitized) text officially circulated.[5]

Is the divide permanent?

If a man of Peter Hain's liberal outlook can speak as he did, are we doomed to the Great Divide between Islam and the West? To a pervasive culture of prejudice and misconceptions, based on cherished stereotypes? The European Union's authoritative race watchdog, the European Monitoring Centre on Racism and Xenophobia, has named leading British newspapers and journals which, it says, contributed to the rise of Islamophobia by sensationalizing cases of Muslim extremism. Even the BBC is not spared, and is criticized for describing Osama bin Laden as an 'Islamic fundamentalist' and an 'Islamic terrorist'. Also in the dock is the former Tory Prime Minister, Margaret Thatcher, for saying that she had not heard 'enough condemnation [of September 11 attacks] from Muslim priests'. While the Centre praises the Prime Minister, Tony Blair, for his swift and strong reaction to Muslim-bashing, it says that by and large, politicians in Britain and mainland Europe have failed to 'adequately address' the issues underlying racism and xenophobia. The prominent British publications which the Centre has particularly blamed for its treatment of Islam and Muslims include *The Daily Telegraph*, *The Sunday Times* and *The Spectator*. A *Sunday Times* columnist has been pulled up for calling British Muslims a 'fifth column in our midst', *The Spectator* gets the rap for a derogatory reference to the Koran, and *The Daily Telegraph* is attacked for seeking to equate Islam with terrorism. The Centre's report lists a series of attacks on Muslims in Britain and other European countries following the September 11 atrocity, and warns the media and politicians against pandering to latent prejudices on the streets. 'By demonizing refugees and asylum seekers you legitimize racism and xenophobia,' the Centre's chairman, Bob Purkiss, said.

John Esposito's latest book reckons with the aftermath of the tragedy of September 11, 2001, when stereotypes and prejudiced generalizations were bruited about with misplaced assurance. He writes: 'Sadly, more than a decade later [after the Gulf War], the same questions about Islam and the Muslim world are still being asked: Why do they hate us? Why is Islam more militant than other religions? What does the Quran have to say about jihad or holy war? Does the Quran condone this kind of violence and terrorism? Is there a clash of civilizations between the West and the Muslim world? . . .

'The Muslim world is no longer "out there". The Muslims are our neighbors, colleagues, and fellow citizens, and their religion, like Judaism and Christianity, rejects terrorism. Never before have soft phrases like "building bridges of understanding" been more critical in a war that ultimately cannot be won simply by military power. Understanding and action go hand in hand for Muslims and non-Muslims alike. All of us are challenged to move beyond stereotypes, historic grievances, and religious differences, to recognize our shared values as well as interests, and to move collectively to build our common future.'[6]

Esposito explains how and why Osama bin Laden rejected a life of wealth and comfort to become a terrorist. The French scholar Olivier Roy uses an apt expression for the credo bin Laden represents: 'The expression of a maverick fundamentalism strangely unfitted for the contemporary world *ummah* (community of the faithful) they think they embody'.[7]

To Olivier Roy goes the credit for predicting that the so-called Islamic fundamentalism had no future and its Afghan variety was bent on self-destruction. It lacks intellectual coherence, is morally blinded and socially perverse. Its appeal, seemingly universal, is rooted in specific situations. 'Militant groups have been especially active in Uzbekistan and Tajikistan, *whose governments have been the most repressive'*.[8]

Esposito mentions another 'Centre' of Islamic fundamentalism: 'Russian President Vladimir Putin provided a vivid example of the exploitation of the rhetoric of "Islamic threat" when he used the spectre of Wahhabi fundamentalism and Taliban-trained mujahideen in the Caucasus to justify launching a war to reassert Russian authority over Chechnya. A veteran human rights activist who visited Grozny, the capital of Chechnya, early in the war disputed the charges, dismissing official Russian accounts as a "monstrous lie" and was equally dismissive of the claims that three hundred Afghan mujahideen fought fiercely against the Russian troops in Grozny. Visiting all the places in Grozny where the Russian government claimed there were Afghan mujahideen, he found no evidence of their presence.

'Chechnya's president Aslan Maskhadov also used the threat

of Wahhabism to crack down on domestic political opposition. In an October 1998 speech before the Congress of the Chechen People, President Maskhadov repudiated Wahhabism as an unwelcome import preached in Chechnya by foreigners, alien to Chechnya's traditional Islam, and responsible for acts of violence. The actual size and threat of radical Wahhabi-inspired movement is hotly contested and difficult to verify.'[9]

Time for the Greater Jihad

No single cause fuelled Muslim rage as much as the establishment of Israel. No other wrong stirs the Arab and the Muslim world as much as the brutal repression by Israel. The extreme and abiding relevance of certain contemporary political situations for stoking the popularity of extremist movements, which invoke the name of Islam, cannot be underestimated. Israel's existence, its suppression of Palestinians and the support it draws from the United States – now the sole superpower – provoke extremism because efforts for compromise, based on recognition of Israel, have failed; the United States makes no pretence of impartiality and its media have little room for any other viewpoint.

It would be suicidal for the Muslim world to allow these trends to affect its sanity. Now, more than ever, is the time for the Greater Jihad – the jihad against ignorance and the evils within Muslim society – while fighting to secure justice. It has fallen to Sayyed Mohammad Khatami, President of the Islamic Republic of Iran, to give a stirring call for a 'Dialogue among civilizations and the World of Islam', a 'Dialogue between East and West'. These are themes of lectures he delivered in recent years. He is very much alive to the treatment of the Third World as a whole, irrespective of the religious divide, but sees no way out of the impasse except through dialogue, in an effort to understand and shed prejudice.

'The two world wars have been the bloodiest of the present grievous state. These two wars occurred in the West, at the hands of Westerners. The infringements on the rights of human beings throughout the world have occurred outside the world of Islam. The rights of the peoples of the continents of Asia, Africa and South America, especially the oppressed people of Palestine, have been trampled upon. This inequality has been imposed even upon non-Muslim countries which were not among industrial nations. With this description, at the end of a century full of blood, war and turmoil, the onset of the third Christian millennium, under the umbrella of "Dialogue and understanding", augurs a brighter and more promising future for mankind. . . . We believe in ratio-nality and dialogue. Religion and history have taught us this lesson.'[10]

It is not one of the 'modernist' Muslim leaders but the President of the Islamic Republic of Iran who asked Muslims to study and reflect, and practise the jihad of reason, ijtihad. 'Which Divine Book or Message more than the Quran has so much emphasized reasoning, meditation, reflection, contemplation, and deliberation on existence and on the world, and on learning from the fate of past peoples and communities? . . . We Muslims believe that we must maintain our faith in the Qur'an and authentic Islam while searching for new answers to today's questions on the basis of religion. The products of Western civilization are everywhere, but I believe that this civilization, too, is not ultimate because it is a human construct.'[11]

Khatami turns the searchlight inwards, on the Muslims them-selves. 'Rectitude is one of the pillars of all religions, especially Islam, and we need a specific interpretation of the term. Unfortunately the idea of rectitude in the history of Islam has been limited to the realm of the individual, the only people who were allowed to govern were the powerful, while the people were kept away from the reins of power. Social rectitude has no precedent in our history. The same Muslims who believed in rectitude committed many social injustices in the Muslim world, and individual rectitude has not been able to overturn these inequities.

'Thus if we say that we possess rectitude and the West does not, we have to know exactly what we mean by rectitude. To religious believers, the relationship between God and humans is clear, *but the relationship of subjects to their rulers, individuals to their society, and various constituents of society to one another have not been scrutinized deeply enough to enable us to know the requirements of this-worldly rectitude.*'

No dialogue will be fruitful unless each side embarks on it with an open mind and after genuine introspection. The West would do well to reflect on the inequities it imposed and continues still to impose on the world, especially on the Muslim countries, and its systematic propagation of falsehoods about Islam and Muslims, despite a growing recognition within Western society of both the inequities and the falsehoods.

Muslims will do themselves no good and much harm were they to wallow in memories of grave wrongs, seek comfort in apologia, turn a blind eye to the injustices in Muslim society and, worst of all, refuse to discard their monstrously wrong notions of their own majestic faith, Islam.

We all need to move on the path of a dialogue among civilizations, which President Khatami advocated with stirring eloquence and transparent sincerity.

On April 28, 1945, on the eve of the outbreak of the Cold War, Winston Churchill pleaded with Joseph Stalin in these prophetic words: 'There is not much comfort in looking into a future where you and the countries you dominate, plus the Communist parties in many other States, are all drawn up on one side, and those who rally to the English-speaking nations and their Associates of Dominions are on the other. It is quite obvious that their quarrel would tear the world to pieces and that all of us leading men on either side who had anything to do with that would be shamed before history'.[12]

Adapt this moving passage to the historic conflict between the West and Islam as it enters the new millennium, and one realizes what a challenge to reflection and creativity we face today.

APPENDICES

1. Universal Islamic Declaration of Human Rights

Prepared by the Islamic Council in Paris on September 19, 1981.
References from the Quran and the Hadith were cited in support of each
provision where necessary.

I. Right to Life
   a. Human life is sacred and inviolable and every effort shall be
   made to protect it. In particular no one shall be exposed to
   injury or death, except under the authority of the Law.
   b. Just as in life, so also after death, the sanctity of a person's
   body shall be inviolable. It is the obligation of believers to see
   that a deceased person's body is handled with due solemnity.

II. Right to Freedom
   a. Man is born free. No inroads shall be made on his right to
   liberty except under the authority and in due process of the
   law.
   b. Every individual and every people has the inalienable right
   to freedom in all its forms – physical, cultural, economic
   and political – and shall be entitled to struggle by all
   available means against any infringement or abrogation of
   this right; and every oppressed individual or people has a
   legitimate claim to the support of other individuals and/or
   peoples in such a struggle.

III. Right to Equality and Prohibition Against Impermissible Discrimination

    a. All persons are equal before the Law and are entitled to equal opportunities and protection of the Law.

    b. All persons shall be entitled to equal wage for equal work.

    c. No person shall be denied the opportunity to work or be discriminated against in any manner or exposed to greater physical risk by reason of religious belief, colour, race, origin, sex or language.

IV. Right to Justice

    a) Every person has the right to be treated in accordance with the Law, and only in accordance with the Law.

    b) Every person has not only the right but also the obligation to protest against injustice; to have recourse to remedies provided by the Law in respect of any unwarranted personal injury or loss; to self-defence against any charges that are preferred against him and to obtain fair adjudication before an independent judicial tribunal in any dispute with public authorities or any other person.

    c) It is the right and duty of every person to defend the rights of any other person and the community in general (*Hisbah*).

    d) No person shall be discriminated against while seeking to defend private and public rights.

    e) It is the right and duty of every Muslim to refuse to obey any command which is contrary to the Law, no matter by whom it may be issued.

V. Right to Fair Trial

    a) No person shall be adjudged guilty of an offence and made liable to punishment except after proof of his guilt before an independent judicial tribunal.

    b) No person shall be adjudged guilty except after a fair trial and after reasonable opportunity for defence has been provided to him.

c) Punishment shall be awarded in accordance with the Law, in proportion to the seriousness of the offence and with due consideration of the circumstances under which it was committed.

d) No act shall be considered a crime unless it is stipulated as such in the clear wording of the Law.

e) Every individual is responsible for his actions. Responsibility for a crime cannot be vicariously extended to other members of his family or group, who are not otherwise directly or indirectly involved in the commission of the crime in question.

VI. Right to Protection Against Abuse of Power

Every person has the right to protection against harassment by official agencies. He is not liable to account for himself except for making a defence to the charges made against him or where he is found in a situation wherein a question regarding suspicion of his involvement in a crime could be *reasonably* raised.

VII. Right to Protection Against Torture

No person shall be subjected to torture in mind or body, or degraded, or threatened with injury either to himself or to anyone related to or held dear by him, or forcibly made to confess to the commission of a crime, or forced to consent to an act which is injurious to his interests.

VIII. Right to Protection of Honour and Reputation

Every person has the right to protect his honour and reputation against calumnies, groundless charges or deliberate attempts at defamation and blackmail.

IX. Right to Asylum

a) Every persecuted or oppressed person has the right to seek refuge and asylum. This right is guaranteed to every human being irrespective of race, religion, colour and sex.

b) Al Masjid Al Haram (the sacred house of Allah) in Mecca is a sanctuary for all Muslims.

X. Rights of Minorities

a) The Quranic principle 'There is no compulsion in religion' shall govern the religious rights of non-Muslim minorities.

b) In a Muslim country religious minorities shall have the choice to be governed in respect of their civil and personal matters by Islamic Law, or by their own laws.

XI. Right and Obligation to Participate in the Conduct and Management of Public Affairs

a) Subject to the Law, every individual in the community (*Ummah*) is entitled to assume public office.

b) Process of free consultation (*Shura*) is the basis of the administrative relationship between the government and the people. People also have the right to choose and remove their rulers in accordance with this principle.

XII. Right to Freedom of Belief, Thought and Speech

a) Every person has the right to express his thoughts and beliefs so long as he remains within the limits prescribed by the Law. No one, however, is entitled to disseminate falsehood or to circulate reports which may outrage public decency, or to indulge in slander, innuendo or to cast defamatory aspersions on other persons.

b) Pursuit of knowledge and search after truth is not only a right but a duty of every Muslim.

c) It is the right and duty of every Muslim to protest and strive (within the limits set out by the Law) against oppression even if it involves challenging the highest authority in the state.

d) There shall be no bar on the dissemination of information provided it does not endanger the security of the society or the state and is confined within the limits imposed by the Law.

e) No one shall hold in contempt or ridicule the religious beliefs of others or incite public hostility against them; respect for the religious feelings of others is obligatory on all Muslims.

XIII. Right to Freedom of Religion
Every person has the right to freedom of conscience and worship in accordance with his religious beliefs.

XIV. Right to Free Association
a) Every person is entitled to participate individually and collectively in the religious, social, cultural and political life of his community and to establish institutions and agencies meant to enjoin what is right (*ma'roof*) and to prevent what is wrong (*munkar*).

b) Every person is entitled to strive for the establishment of institutions whereunder an enjoyment of these rights would be made possible. Collectively, the community is obliged to establish conditions so as to allow its members full development of their personalities.

XV. The Economic Order and the Rights Evolving Therefrom
a) In their economic pursuits, all persons are entitled to the full benefits of nature and all its resources. These are blessings bestowed by God for the benefit of mankind as a whole.

b) All human beings are entitled to earn their living according to the Law.

c) Every person is entitled to own property individually or in association with others. State ownership of certain economic resources in the public interest is legitimate.

d) The poor have the right to a prescribed share in the wealth of the rich, as fixed by Zakat, levied and collected in accordance with the Law.

e) All means of production shall be utilized in the interest of the community (*Ummah*) as a whole, and may not be neglected or misused.

f) In order to promote the development of a balanced economy and to protect society from exploitation, Islamic Law forbids monopolies, unreasonable restrictive trade practices, usury, the use of coercion in the making of contracts and the publication of misleading advertisements.

g) All economic activities are permitted provided they are not detrimental to the interests of the community (*Ummah*) and do not violate Islamic laws and values.

XVI. Right to Protection of Property
No property may be expropriated except in the public interest and on payment of fair and adequate compensation.

XVII. Status and Dignity of Workers
Islam honours work and the workers and enjoins Muslims not only to treat the worker justly but also generously. He is not only to be paid his earned wages promptly, but is also entitled to adequate rest and leisure.

XVIII. Right to Social Security
Every person has the right to food, shelter, clothing, education and medical care consistent with the resources of

the community. This obligation of the community extends in particular to all individuals who cannot take care of themselves due to some temporary or permanent disability.

XIX. Right to Found a Family and Related Matters
   a) Every person is entitled to marry, to found a family and to bring up children in conformity with his religion, traditions and culture. Every spouse is entitled to such rights and privileges and carries such obligations as are stipulated by the Law.
   b) Each of the partners in a marriage is entitled to respect and consideration from the other.
   c) Every husband is obligated to maintain his wife and children according to his means.
   d) Every child has the right to be maintained and properly brought up by its parents, it being forbidden that children are made to work at an early age or that any burden is put on them which would arrest or harm their natural development.
   e) If parents are for some reason unable to discharge their obligations towards a child it becomes the responsibility of the community to fulfill these obligations at public expense.
   f) Every person is entitled to material support, as well as care and protection, from his family during his childhood, old age or incapacity. Parents are entitled to material support as well as care and protection from their children.
   g) Motherhood is entitled to special respect, care and assistance on the part of the family and the public organs of the community (*Ummah*).
   h) Within the family, men and women are to share in their obligations and responsibilities according to their sex, their natural endowments, talents and inclinations, bearing in

mind their common responsibilities toward their progeny and their relatives.

i) No person may be married against his or her will, or lose or suffer diminution of legal personality on account of marriage.

XX. Rights of Married Women

Every married woman is entitled to:

a) Receive the means necessary for maintaining a standard of living which is not inferior to that of her spouse, and, in the event of divorce, receive during the statutory period of waiting (*Iddah*) means of maintenance commensurate with her husband's resources, for herself as well as for the children she nurses or keeps, irrespective of her own financial status, earnings, or property that she may hold in her own right.

b) Seek and obtain dissolution of marriage (*Khul'a*) in accordance with the terms of the Law. This right is in addition to her right to seek divorce through the courts.

c) Inherit from her husband, her parents, her children and other relatives according to the Law.

d) Strict confidentiality from her spouse, or ex-spouse if divorced, with regard to any information that he may have obtained about her, the disclosure of which could prove detrimental to her interests. A similar responsibility rests upon her in respect of her spouse or ex-spouse.

XXI. Right to Education

a) Every person is entitled to receive education in accordance with his natural capabilities.

b) Every person is entitled to a free choice of profession and career and to the opportunity for the full development of his natural endowments.

XXII. Right of Privacy

Every person is entitled to the protection of his privacy.

XXIII. Right to Freedom of Movement and Residence

a) In view of the fact that the World of Islam is veritably *Ummah Islamia*, every Muslim shall have the right to freely move in and out of any Muslim country.

b) No one shall be forced to leave the country of his residence, or be arbitrarily deported therefrom, without recourse to due process of Law.

EXPLANATORY NOTES

1. In the above formulation of Human Rights, unless the context provides otherwise:

a) The term 'person' refers to both the male and female sexes.

b) The term 'Law' denotes the *Shari'ah*, i.e. the totality of ordinances derived from the Qur'an and the Sunnah and any other laws that are deduced from these two sources by methods considered valid in Islamic jurisprudence.

2. Each one of the Human Rights enunciated in this Declaration carries a corresponding duty.

3. In the exercise and enjoyment of the rights referred to above every person shall be subject only to such limitations as are enjoined by the Law for the purpose of securing the due recognition of, and respect for, the rights and the freedom of others and of meeting the just requirements of morality, public order and the general welfare of the Community (*Ummah*).

4. The Arabic text of this *Declaration* is the original.

2. The Protection of Human Rights
in Islamic Criminal Justice

The First International Conference on 'The Protection of Human Rights in Islamic Criminal Justice' took place at the International Institute of Advanced Criminal Sciences in Siracusa, Italy, May 28–31, 1979, under the chairmanship of Professors M. Cherif Bassiouni and Ahmad Fathi Sorour. In attendance were 55 jurists, mostly panellists, from 18 countries. (Among them were officials from Egypt, Syria, Libya, Saudi Arabia, UAE, Algeria, Somalia, Mauritania, Jordan, Sudan, as well as scholars from the US, France, Italy, Belgium, Yugoslavia, the UK, and Switzerland.) The four-day conference heard and discussed reports on substantive crimes in Islamic law, the development of criminal codification, criminal procedure, the rights of accused in the criminal justice system, and penalties. At the conclusion of the conference the participants voted unanimously (with one abstention) this resolution which embodies those standards of criminal justice which are in harmony, if not in conformity, with guarantees embodied in internationally protected human rights. The text reproduced here is from *The Islamic Criminal Justice System*, edited by M. Cherif Bassiouni, Oceana Publications, New York 1982.

RESOLUTION

Whereas the First International Conference on the Protection of Human Rights in the Islamic Criminal Justice System has been held in Siracusa, Italy, at the International Institute of Higher Studies in Criminal Sciences, May 28–31, 1979;

Whereas it has been established to the satisfaction of all participants from both Islamic and non-Islamic nations that the letter and spirit of Islamic Law on the subject of the protection of the rights of the criminally accused are in complete harmony with the fundamental principles of human rights under international law as well as in complete harmony with the respect accorded to the equality and dignity of all persons under the constitutions and laws of Muslim and non-Muslim nations of the world;

Whereas the basic human rights embodied in the principles of Islamic Law include the following rights of the criminally accused, inter alia:

1. the right of freedom from arbitrary arrest, detention, torture, or physical annihilation;
2. the right to be presumed innocent until proven guilty by a fair and impartial tribunal in accordance with the Rule of Law;
3. the application of the Principle of Legality which calls for the right of the accused to be tried for crimes specified in the Qu'ran or other crimes whose clear and well-established meaning and content are determined by Shariah Law (Islamic Law) or by a criminal code in conformity therewith;
4. the right to appear before an appropriate tribunal previously established by law;
5. the right to a public trial;
6. the right not to be compelled to testify against oneself;
7. the right to present evidence and to call witnesses in one's defense;
8. the right to counsel of one's own choosing;
9. the right to a decision on the merits based upon legally admissible evidence;
10. the right to have the decision in the case rendered in public;
11. the right to benefit from the spirit of Mercy and the goals of

rehabilitation and resocialization in the consideration of the
penalty to be imposed; and

12. the right of appeal.

Whereas the aforementioned rights of due process of law
contained in Islamic Law are in complete harmony with the prescriptions of the International Covenant on Civil and Political
Rights which has been signed or ratified by many nations
including a significant number of Muslim and Islamic nations and
which reflects generally accepted principles of international law
contained in the Universal Declaration of Human rights of 1948,
and the U.N. Declaration on the Standard Minimum Rules for
the Treatment of Offenders;

Now therefore the participants of the Conference in their
individual capacities, desirous of upholding the aforementioned
principles and the values they embody, and desirous of ensuring
that the practices and procedures of Islamic and Muslim nations
conform thereto, solemnly declare that:

Any departure from the aforementioned principles would
constitute a serious and grave violation of Shariah Law, international human rights law, and the generally accepted principles of
international law reflected in the constitutions and laws of most
nations of the world.

Siracusa, May 31, 1979

NOTES

1. Introduction – 'The Spectre of Islam'

1 *Time*, February 25, 1991.
2 'Is Islam an Enemy of the United States?', *New Hampshire Sunday News*, November 25, 1990.
3 John L. Esposito, *The Islamic Threat: Myth or Reality?*, Oxford University Press, 3rd edition 1998.
4 Samuel P. Huntington, *The Clash of Civilizations and the Remaking of World Order*, Penguin Books 1997.
5 Ibid., pp. 217–18.
6 Ibid., p. 209.
7 Esposito, *The Islamic Threat*, p. 44.
8 Ibid., Preface to the Third Edition, p. ix.
9 Mark Huband, *Warriors of the Prophet: The Struggle for Islam*, Westview Press 1999, p. 58.
10 Ibid., p. 59.
11 John K. Cooley, *Unholy Wars*, Pluto Press 2000, p. 120.
12 Ibid.
13 *The Herald*, November 2001.
14 *The Economist*, December 8, 2000.
15 *International Herald Tribune*, December 7, 2001.
16 *The Economist*, September 15, 2001, p. 5.
17 Ibid., p. 8.
18 *The Economist*, September 22, 2001, p. 10.
19 *The Economist*, October 6, 2001.

20 Edward Said, 'The Campaign against "Islamic Terror"', March 1996, reproduced in Said, *The End of the Peace Process*, Granta Books 2000, p. 45.

21 Edward Said, *The Politics of Dispossession*, Vintage Books 1995, pp. 388–89.

22 *Islamism and Security: Political Islam and the Western World*, edited by Frédéric Grare, Programme for Strategic and International Security Studies, The Graduate Institute of International Studies, Geneva 1999, p. 18.

23 *The Asian Age*, December 24, 1997.

24 See Ilan Pappé (ed.), *The Israel/Palestine Question: Rewriting Histories*, Routledge 1999.

25 Tom Segev, *One Palestine, Complete: Jews and Arabs Under the British Mandate*, Little, Brown and Company 2000.

26 Ibid., p. 496.

27 Shabbir Akhtar, *The Final Imperative*, Bellew Publishing, London 1991, pp. 4–5.

28 See the author's *The RSS and the BJP: A Division of Labour*, LeftWord Books 2001.

29 Susanne Hoeber Rudolph and Lloyd I. Rudolph, 'Modern Hate', *The New Republic*, March 22, 1993.

30 *Organiser*, November 4, 2001.

31 M.S. Golwalkar, *Bunch of Thoughts*, Vikrama Prakashan, Bangalore 1968, p. 148.

32 *The Statesman*, April 28, 1991.

33 Tapan Basu, Pradip Datta, Sumit Sarkar, Tanika Sarkar and Sambuddha Sen, *Khaki Shorts, Saffron Flags*, Orient Longman 1993, pp. 4–5.

34 Romila Thapar, *Interpreting Early India*, Oxford University Press 1993, p. 86.

2. The Long March of Prejudice

1 Edward Gibbon, *The Decline and Fall of the Roman Empire*, The Modern Library, New York 1781, Vol. II, p. 801.

2 Minou Reeves, *Muhammad in Europe: A Thousand Years of Western Myth-Making*, New York University Press 2000.

3 Ibid., p. 242.

4 Ibid., p. 247.

5 *The New York Times*, June 1, 1919, quoted in John L. Esposito, *The Islamic Threat*, p. 222.

6 Sushil Srivastava, *The Disputed Mosque: A Historical Inquiry*, Vistaar 1991, p. 27.
7 Minou Reeves, *Muhammad in Europe*, pp. 81–82.
8 Ibid., p. 94.
9 Karen Armstrong, *Muhammad: A Biography of the Prophet*, Victor Gollancz 1995.
10 Ibid., pp. 10–11.
11 Reeves, *Muhammad in Europe*, p. 113.
12 Ibid., p. 300.
13 Edward Said, *Orientalism*, Vintage 1979, p. 278.
14 Edward Said, *Covering Islam*, Vintage 1997, p. 9.
15 In this case the Jewish magazine *Commentary*.
16 Bernard Lewis, 'The Roots of Muslim Rage', *Atlantic Monthly*, September 1990. Samuel P. Huntington, 'The Clash of Civilizations', *Foreign Affairs*, Summer 1993.
17 John L. Esposito, *The Islamic Threat*, p. 220.
18 Ziauddin Sardar, *Orientalism*, Open University Press 1999, p. 69.
19 Edward Said, *Covering Islam*, p. xxxii.
20 November 25, 1979.
21 Edward Said, *Covering Islam*, p. 114.
22 Daya Kishen Thussu, 'How Media Manipulates Truth about Terrorism', *Economic and Political Weekly*, February 8, 1997.
23 *The Spectator*, October 19, 1991.

3. The Meanings of Jihad and Fatwa

1 *Al Fath at Kabir*, vol. I, p. 208.
2 Roland E. Miller, *Muslim Friends: Their Faith and Feeling. An Introduction to Islam*, Orient Longman 2000, pp. 245–46.
3 Ibid., p. 253.
4 Ibid., p. 254.
5 Bruce B. Lawrence, *Shattering the Myth: Islam Beyond Violence*, Oxford University Press 2000, p. 182.
6 Ibid., p. 159.
7 Ibid., p. 185.
8 Ibid., p. 176.
9 Ibid., p. 177.
10 Karen Armstrong, *Muhammad: A Biography of the Prophet*, pp. 165–68.

11 Ibid, p. 168.

12 Sayed Abdullah S.M., 'Islamic Concept of Jihad and Tolerance', *Radiance Viewsweekly*, November 25, 2001.

13 Maulvi Chiragh Ali, *A Critical Exposition of the Popular 'Jihad'*, Idarah-i-Adabiyati Dilli, reprint Delhi 1984.

14 See Supplement to the Gazette of India, April 21, 1883, page 807.

15 Aziz Ahmad, *Islamic Modernism in India and Pakistan 1857–1964*, Oxford University Press 1967, p. 57.

16 Maulvi Chiragh Ali, *A Critical Exposition*, pp. xxiv–xxv.

17 *Organiser*, November 4, 2001.

18 Sura 8: Verse 39.

19 *The Message of The Quran*, translated and explained by Muhammad Asad, Dar Al-Andalus, Gibraltar 1980, p. 244.

20 Sura 9-5.

21 Clinton Bennett, *In Search of Muhammad*, Cassell 1998.

22 Ibid., p. 119. The references for the quotes are as follows: Fred Doner, 'The Sources of Islamic Conceptions of War', in John Kelsay and James Turner Johnson (eds.), *Just War and Jihad: Historical and Theoretical Perspectives on Peace and War in Western and Islamic Traditions*, Greenwood Press, New York 1991, p. 47; Afzalur Rahman, *Muhammad as a Military Leader*, The Muslim Schools Trust, London 1980, p. 279; Muhammad Ali, *The Living Thoughts of the Prophet Muhammad*, Castle, London 1948, p. 34; Martin Forward, *Muhammad: A Short Biography*, Oxford One World, 1997, p. 27.

23 Asad, *The Message of The Quran*, p. 256.

24 Maulvi Chiragh Ali, *A Critical Exposition*, p. 129.

25 Ibid., p. 134.

26 Ibid., p. 138.

27 Ibid., p. lii.

28 *The Economist*, November 24, 2001.

29 *Terrorising the Truth: The Shaping of Contemporary Images of Islam and Muslim in Media, Politics and Culture*, prepared by Dr. Farish A. Noor, JUST, Penang, 1997.

30 Chaiwat Satha-Anand (Qader Muheideen), 'The Non-violent Crescent: Eight Theses on Muslim Non-violent Actions', ibid., p. 166.

31 Christian W. Troll, 'Abul Kalam Azad's Sarmad the Martyr' in Christopher Shackle (ed.) *Urdu and Muslim South Asia*, School of Oriental and African Studies, London 1989, p.124.

32 Barbara Metcalf, *Islamic Revival in British India: Deobana, 1860–1900*, Princeton University Press 1982, pp. 50 and 146.

4. The Very Modern Roots of Islamic Fundamentalism

1   Karen Armstrong, *Muhammad*, p. 11.
2   Karen Armstrong, *The Battle for God*, Alfred A. Knopf, New York 2000, p.ix.
3   *Asian Age*, December 16, 2001.
4   See the author's book *The RSS and the BJP: A Division of Labour*, LeftWord Books, New Delhi 2001.
5   *Asian Age*, December 24, 2001.
6   See Sayyid A.S. Pirazada, *The Politics of the Jamiat Ulema-I-Islam Pakistan 1971–77*, Oxford University Press, Karachi 2000, pp. 234–35.
7   M.S. Golwalkar, *A Bunch of Thoughts*, p. 2.
8   Karen Armstrong, *Islam: A Short History*, Phoenix Press, London 2001, p.141.
9   John L. Esposito, *The Islamic Threat: Myth or Reality?*, Oxford University Press, 1999, p. 5.
10 Bernard Lewis, *Foreign Affairs*, October 1992, p. 115.
11 Malise Ruthven, *Islam: A Very Short Introduction*, Oxford University Press 1997, p. 21.
12 Karen Armstrong, *The Battle for God*, p. 220.
13 Malise Ruthven, *Islam*, p. 131.
14 Frédéric Grare, *Political Islam in the Indian Subcontinent: The Jamaat-I-Islami*, Manohar and Centre de Sciences Humaines, New Delhi 2002, p. 18.
15 Karen Armstrong, *The Battle for God*, pp. 238–40.
16 Ibid., p. 240.
17 Ibid., p. 243.
18 Karen Armstrong, *Islam: A Short History*, p. 143.
19 *Report of the Court of Inquiry constituted under the Punjab Act 11 of 1954 to enquire into the Punjab Disturbances of 1953*, Lahore, Superintendent Government Printing, Punjab 1954 (popularly known as the Munir Report), p. 203
20 *Milestones*, p. 115; quoted in Patrick Bannerman, *Islam in Perspective: A Guide to Islamic Society, Politics and Law*, Routledge for the Royal Institute of International Affairs, London 1988, p. 149.
21 Maulana Abul A'la Maududi, *The Islamic Law and Constitution*, translated and edited by Khurshid Ahmad, Islamic Publications, Lahore 1967, p. 175.
22 Munir Report, p. 232.
23 Ibn Khaldun, *The Muqaddimahi: An Introduction to History*, translated from the Arabic by Franz Rosenthal, abridged and edited by N.J. Dawood,

Princeton University Press 1974, p. 169.

24 Muhammad Asad, *The Message of the Quran*, p. 512.

25 Maulana Abul A'la Maududi, *The Islamic Law and Constitution*, p. 283.

26 Qamaruddin Khan, *Al-Mawardi's Theory of the State*, Bazm-i-Iqbal, Lahore, n.d.

27 Ibid., pp. 37 and 39.

28 Muhammad Heikal, *The Illusion of Triumph*, Harper Collins 1992, p. 54.

29 Tom Segev, *One Palestine, Complete*, Little, Brown and Company 2000, p. 496.

30 Ibid., p. 56.

31 Muhammad Heikal, *The Illusion of Triumph*, p. 57.

32 Ibid., p. 58.

33 Detlev H. Khalid, 'Phenomenon of Re-Islamization', *Aussenpolitik*, Vol. 29, No. 4.

34 Ibid., p. 448.

35 Mark Huband, *Warriors of the Prophet*, p. 194.

36 Olivier Roy, *The Failure of Political Islam*, I.B. Tauris Publishers, London 1994, pp. 195–97.

37 *Asian Age*, November 10, 2001.

38 Poornima Joshi, *The Hindustan Times*, November 11, 2001.

39 *Radiance Viewsweekly*, November 18, 2001.

40 *The Hindu*, November 11, 2001.

41 Quoted in Edward Said, *The Politics of Dispossession*, Vintage Books, New York 1995, p. 388.

5. Human Rights in the Islamic Tradition

1 Count Leon Ostrorog, *The Angora Reform*, London 1927, pp. 30–31.

2 M. Muhammad Ubaidul Akbar, *The Orations of Muhammad: The Prophet of Islam*, Kitab Bhavan, New Delhi 1981, p. 96.

3 *Muhammad: Prophet and Statesman*, Oxford University Press 1961, p. 228.

4 A. Guillaume, *The Life of Muhammad: A Translation of Ibn Ishaq's Sirat Rasul Allah*, Oxford University Press 1978, pp. 683 and 687.

5 Muhammad Hamid Ansari, *Islam and Democracy*, p. 11. The writer is indebted to Ansari for this summary.

6 Muddathir Abd al-Rahim, *Islam and Non-Muslim Minorities*, Just World Trust 1997, p. 7.

7 Sheikh Showkat Hussain, *Minorities: Islam and the Nation-State*, Islamic

Book Trust, Kuala Lumpur 1997, p. 60.

8 Muhammad Talat Ghunaymi, *The Muslim Conception of International Law and the Western Approach*, The Hague 1968; cited in ibid., p. 25.

9 Ibid., p. 32.

10 Ibid., p. 33.

11 Maulana Abul A'la Maududi, *Human Rights in Islam*, The Islamic Foundation, London 1980, p. 21.

12 Maulana Abul A'la Maududi, *Islamic Law and Constitution*, p. 55.

13 Hakim Abdul Hameed (ed.), *Islam at a Glance*, Indian Institute of Islamic Studies and Vikas, New Delhi 1981, pp. 76–89; present quotation on p. 83.

14 Asghar Ali Engineer, *Islam and its Relevance to our Age*, Institute of Islamic Studies, Mumbai 1984; see the essay 'Developing Liberation Theology in Islam', pp. 88–129.

15 Ibid., p. 111.

16 Ibid., p. 123.

6. Ijtihad (Reason) and the Challenge of Modernity

1 The Munir Report, p. 232.

2 *International Herald Tribune*, November 30, 2001.

3 Ralph Russell and Khurshidul Islam, *Ghalib: Life and Letters*, Oxford University Press 1969, p. 273.

4 Nikki R. Keddie, *An Islamic Response to Imperialism*, University of California Press 1968.

5 Jawaharlal Nehru, *The Discovery of India*, Jawaharlal Nehru Memorial Fund and Oxford University Press 1946, p. 345.

6 Nikki R. Keddie, *An Islamic Response to Imperialism*, p. 61.

7 Ibid., p. 62.

8 Ibid., p. 64.

9 Ibid., p. 70.

10 Maulvi Chiragh Ali, *The Proposed Political, Legal and Social Reforms under Moslem Rule*, Bombay Education Society Press 1883.

11 Maulvi Chiragh Ali, *A Critical Exposition of the Popular 'Jihad'*, pp. 159–60.

12 Iqbal, *The Reconstruction of Religious Thought in Islam*, 1930.

13 Ibid., p. 164.

14 Ibid., p. 168.

15 Muhammad Sadiq, *A History of Urdu Literature*, Oxford University Press

1994, p. 460.

16 Fazlur Rahman, *Islam and Modernity: Transformation of an Intellectual Tradition*, The University of Chicago Press 1982, p. 141.

17 Shabbir Akhtar, *A Faith for All Seasons: Islam and the Challenge of the Modern World*, Ivan R. Dee, Chicago, 1990.

18 Bruce B. Lawrence, *Shattering the Myth*, p. 101.

19 Syeda Saiyidain Hameed (ed.), *India's Maulana: Abul Kalam Azad*, Indian Council for Cultural Relations and Vikas, New Delhi 1990, Vol. II, pp. 66–8.

7. Epilogue: Time for the Greater Jihad

1 Peter Hain, *Political Trials in Britain*, Penguin Books 1984.

2 *The Sunday Times*, May 13, 2002.

3 *The Guardian*, May 13, 2002.

4 *The Hindu*, May 13, 2002.

5 *The Telegraph*, May 17, 2002.

6 John L. Esposito, *Unholy War: Terror in the Name of Islam*, Oxford University Press 2002, pp. ix and xi.

7 Olivier Roy, 'Has Islamism a Future', in *Afghanistan and the Taliban: The Rebirth of Fundamentalism?*, edited by William Maley, Penguin Books 2001, p. 211.

8 John L. Esposito, *Unholy War*, p. 112; see also Ahmed Rashid, *Jihad: The Rise of Militant Islam in Central Asia*, Orient Longman 2002.

9 Ibid., pp. 114–15.

10 Mohammad Khatami, *Islam, Dialogue and Civil Society*, Centre for Arab and Islamic Studies (The Muslim East and Central Asia), The Australian National University, Canberra 2000, pp. 1–2.

11 Ibid., pp. 19 and 37.

12 *Correspondence Between the Chairman of the Council of Ministers of the USSR and the Presidents of the USA and the Prime Ministers of Great Britain During the Great Patriotic War of 1941–1945*, Volume 1, Foreign Languages Publishing House, Moscow 1957, p. 343.

SELECT
BIBLIOGRAPHY

Abd al-Rahim, Muddathir 1997. *Islam and Non-Muslim Minorities*, Just World Trust

Abdullah, Sayed S.M. 2001. 'Islamic Concept of Jihad and Tolerance', *Radiance Viewsweekly*, November 25

Ahmad, Aziz 1967. *Islamic Modernism in India and Pakistan 1857–1964*, Oxford University Press

Akbar, M. Muhammad Ubaidul 1981. *The Orations of Muhammad: The Prophet of Islam*, New Delhi: Kitab Bhavan

Akhtar, Shabbir 1990. *A Faith for All Seasons: Islam and the Challenge of the Modern World*, Chicago, Ivan R. Dee

Akhtar, Shabbir 1991. *The Final Imperative*, London: Bellow Publishing

Ali, Muhammad 1948. *The Living Thoughts of the Prophet Muhammad*, London: Castle

Arberry, Arthur J. 1992. *An Introduction to the History of Sufism*, Sangam Books

Armstrong, Karen 1995. *Muhammad: A Biography of the Prophet*, Victor Gollancz

Armstrong, Karen 2000. *The Battle for God*, New York: Alfred A. Knopf

Armstrong, Karen 2001. *Islam: A Short History*, London: Phoenix Press

Bannerman, Patrick 1988. *Islam in Perspective: A Guide to Islamic Society, Politics and Law*, London: Routledge for the Royal Institute of International Affairs

Basu, Tapan, Pradip Datta, Sumit Sarkar, Tanika Sarkar and Sambuddha Sen, 1993. *Khaki Shorts, Saffron Flags*, New Delhi: Orient Longman

Bennett, Clinton 1998. *In Search of Muhammad*, Cassell

Bloom, Jonathan and Sheila Blair 2002. *Islam: A Thousand Years of Faith and Power*, London: Yale University Press

Chiragh Ali, Maulvi 1883. *The Proposed Political, Legal and Social Reforms under Moslem Rule*, Bombay: Bombay Education Society Press

Chiragh Ali, Maulvi 1984. *A Critical Exposition of the Popular 'Jihad'*, Delhi: Idarah-i-Adabiyati Dilli

Cooley, John K. 2000. *Unholy Wars*, London: Pluto Press

Doner, Fred 1991. 'The Sources of Islamic Conceptions of War' in Kelsay and Turner Johnson 1991

Enan, Muhammad Abdullah 1940. *Decisive Moments in the History of Islam* (English translation of a work published in Arabic in Cairo) Lahore: Shaikh Muhammad Ashraf.

Engineer, Asghar Ali 1984. *Islam and its Relevance to our Age*, Mumbai: Institute of Islamic Studies

Esposito, John L. (ed.) 1983. *Voices of Resurgent Islam*, Oxford University Press

Esposito, John L. 1999. *The Islamic Threat: Myth or Reality?*, Oxford University Press, 3rd edition

Esposito, John L. 2002. *Unholy War: Terror in the Name of Islam*, Oxford University Press

Forward, Martin 1997. *Muhammad: A Short Biography*, Oxford One World

Ghunaymi, Muhammad Talat 1968. *The Muslim Conception of International Law and the Western Approach*, The Hague

Gibbon, Edward 1781. *The Decline and Fall of the Roman Empire*, New York: The Modern Library

Golwalkar, M.S. 1968. *Bunch of Thoughts*, Bangalore: Vikrama Prakashan

Grare, Frédéric (ed.) 1999. *Islamism and Security: Political Islam and the Western World*, Programme for Strategic and International Security Studies, the Graduate Institute of International Studies, Geneva

Grare, Frédéric 2002. *Political Islam in the Indian Subcontinent: The Jamaat-I-Islami*, New Delhi: Manohar and Centre de Sciences Humaines

Guillaume, A. 1978. *The Life of Muhammad: A translation of Ibn Ishaq's Sirat Rasul Allah*, Oxford University Press

Hameed, Hakim Abdul (ed.), 1981. *Islam at a Glance*, New Delhi: Indian Institute of Islamic Studies and Vikas

Heikal, Muhammad 1992. *The Illusion of Triumph*, Harper Collins

Huband, Mark 1999. *Warriors of the Prophet: The Struggle for Islam*, Westview Press

Huntington, Samuel P. 1993. 'The Clash of Civilizations', *Foreign Affairs*, Summer

Huntington, Samuel P. 1997. *The Clash of Civilizations and the Remaking of World Order*, Penguin Books

Hussain, Sheikh Showkat 1997. *Minorities: Islam and the Nation-State*, Kuala Lumpur: Islamic Book Trust

Ibn Khaldun 1974. *The Muqaddimah: An Introduction to History*, translated from the Arabic by Franz Rosenthal, abridged and edited by N.J. Dawood, Princeton University Press

International Commission of Jurists 1982. *Human Rights in Islam*, Geneva: International Commission of Jurists in association with Kuwait University and Union of Arab Lawyers

Iqbal, Muhammad 1930. *The Reconstruction of Religious Thought in Islam*, Lahore

Izetbegovic, Alija Ali 1989. *Islam Between East and West*, Indiana: American Trust Publications

JUST, 1997. *Terrorizing the Truth: The Shaping of Contemporary Images of Islam and*

Muslim in Media, Politics and Culture, prepared by Dr. Farish A. Noor, Penang: JUST

Keddie, Nikki R. 1968. *An Islamic Response to Imperialism*, University of California Press

Kelsay, John and James Turner Johnson (eds.) 1991. *Just War and Jihad: Historical and Theoretical Perspectives on Peace and War in Western and Islamic Traditions*, New York: Greenwood Press

Kerr, Malcolm H. 1966. *Islamic Reform: The Political and Legal Theories of Muhammad Abduh and Rashid Rida*, University of California Press

Khalid, Detlev H. 'Phenomenon of Re-Islamization', *Aussenpolitik*, Vol. 29, No. 4

Khan, Qamaruddin n.d. *Al-Mawardi's Theory of the State*, Lahore: Bazm-i-Iqbal

Kurzman, Charles (ed.) 1998. *Liberal Islam, A Sourcebook*, New York: Oxford University Press

Lawrence, Bruce B. 2000. *Shattering the Myth: Islam Beyond Violence*, Oxford University Press

Lewis, Bernard 1990. 'The Roots of Muslim Rage', *Atlantic Monthly*, September

Maley, William (ed.) 2001. *Afghanistan and the Taliban: The Rebirth of Fundamentalism?*, Penguin Books

Maududi, Maulana Abul A'la 1967. *The Islamic Law and Constitution*, translated and edited by Khurshid Ahmad, Lahore: Islamic Publications

Maududi, Maulana Abul A'la 1980. *Human Rights in Islam*, London: The Islamic Foundation

Mernissi, Fatima 1992. *Islam and Democracy*, Addison Wesley Publishing Company

Mernissi, Fatima 1993. *Women and Islam: An Historical and Theological Enquiry*, Delhi: Kali for Women

Metcalf, Barbara 1982. *Islamic Revival in British India: Deoband 1860–1900*, Princeton University Press

Miller, Roland E. 2000. *Muslim Friends: Their Faith and Feeling. An Introduction to Islam*, New Delhi: Orient Longman

Nehru, Jawaharlal 1946. *The Discovery of India*, reprint by Jawaharlal Nehru Memorial Fund and Oxford University Press

Ostrorog, Count Leon 1927. *The Angora Reform*, London

Pappé, Ilan (ed.) 1999. *The Israel/Palestine Question: Rewriting Histories*, Routledge

Pirazada, Sayyid A.S. 2000. *The Politics of the Jamiat Ulema-I-Islam Pakistan 1971–77*, Karachi: Oxford University Press

Qureshi, Sultan Ahmed (ed). 1986. *Letters of the Holy Prophet*, Delhi: Noor Publishing House

Rahman, Afzalur 1980. *Muhammad as a Military Leader*, London: The Muslim Schools Trust

Rahman, Fazlur 1979. *Islam*, Chicago and London: The University of Chicago Press

Rahman, Fazlur 1982. *Islam & Modernity: Transformation of an Intellectual Tradition*, Chicago and London: The University of Chicago Press

Rashid, Ahmed 2002. *Jihad: The Rise of Militant Islam in Central Asia*, New Delhi: Orient Longman

Reeves, Minou 2000. *Muhammad in Europe: A Thousand Years of Western Myth-Making*, New York University Press

Report of the Court of Inquiry constituted under the Punjab Act 11 of 1954 to enquire into the Punjab Disturbances of 1953, Lahore, Superintendent Government Printing, Punjab 1954 (popularly known as the Munir Report)

Roy, Olivier 1994. *The Failure of Political Islam*, London: I.B. Tauris Publishers

Russell, Ralph and Khurshidul Islam 1969. *Ghalib: Life and Letters*, Oxford University Press

Ruthven, Malise 1997. *Islam: A Very Short Introduction*, Oxford University Press

Ruthven, Malise 2000. *Islam in the World*, Oxford University Press

Sadiq, Muhammad 1994. *A History of Urdu Literature*, Oxford University Press

Said, Edward 1979. *Orientalism*, Vintage Books

Said, Edward 1995. *The Politics of Dispossession*, Vintage Books

Said, Edward 1997. *Covering Islam*, Vintage Books

Said, Edward 2000. *The End of the Peace Process*, Granta Books

Sardar, Ziauddin 1987. *The Future of Muslim Civilization*, London and New York: Mansell Publishing Limited

Sardar, Ziauddin 1999. *Orientalism*, Open University Press

Schimmel, Annemarie 1975. *Mystical Dimensions of Islam*, Chapel Hill: The University of North Carolina Press

Schimmel, Annemarie 1985. *And Muhammad is His Messenger: The Veneration of the Prophet in Islamic Piety*, Chapel Hill: The University of North Carolina Press

Segev, Tom 2000. *One Palestine, Complete: Jews and Arabs Under the British Mandate*, Little, Brown and Company

Smith, Wilfred Cantwell 1957. *Islam in Modern History*, Princeton University Press, 1957

Smith, Wilfred Cantwell 2000. *On Understanding Islam: Selected Studies*, Delhi, Idarah-i Adalbiyat-i Delhi

Srivastava, Sushil 1991. *The Disputed Mosque: A Historical Inquiry*, Vistaar

Thapar, Romila 1993. *Interpreting Early India*, Oxford University Press

The Message of the Quran, translated and explained by Muhammad Asad, Gibraltar: Dar Al-Andalus, 1980

Thussu, Daya Kishen 1997. 'How Media Manipulates Truth about Terrorism', *Economic and Political Weekly*, February 8

Watt, Montgomery 1961. *Muhammad: Prophet and Statesman*, Oxford University Press

INDEX

Goel, Sita Ram, 22
Goethe, Johann, 36,
Golwalkar, M.S., 21, 67
Grare, Frédéric, 71
Grozny, Russian troops, 125
Gulf War, 8

Habash, Georges, 12, 15
hadith, 19, 49, 59, 100, 106, 111
Haifa University, 17
Hain, Peter, 121-3
Hamas, 14, 19
Hamza Khan, Maulvi, 107
Hanafee code, 57
Hargreaves, Ian, 41
Hedaya, 56
Heikal Muhammad, 18, 79, 81
Hezbollah, 13, 84
Hinduism, 50; fundamentalist, 67;
    nationalist, 20-3; radical, 65
Hodgson, Marshal, 15
Hottinger, Arnold, 15
Huband, Mark, 82
Hughes, Simon, 122
Hugo, Victor, 35
human rights, 93; Islamic, 97; Quran, 96
Huntington, Samuel P., 5, 13, 37
Haq, Zia-ul, 18-19, 67
Hussein, Saddam, 4, 18

Ibish, Yusuf, 46
ijtihad, 24, 111-13, 127
India: 1857 mutiny, 14; British rule, 115;
    hate-mongers, 20;
islamophobia, 42; Muslims, 47, 112
Institute of Islamic Research, Karachi,
    113
Iqbal, Muhammad, 24, 94, 108, 111-12
Iran, 4, 57, 84; Islamic Revolution, 6,
    39; revolution, 48, 80; Shah of, 18
Iraq, 89; Kuwait invasion, 4
Islam: criminal justice system, 142-4;
    culture, 15; democratic governance,
    95; democratic ideals, 78-9; funda-
    mentalist, 4, 24, 30-1, 68, 70, 75-6,

80; fundamentalist splits, 82-3;
    images of, 58; Iranian revolution, 6,
    39; liberation theology, 100, 115,
    118; nationalist, 88; non-Arab, 81;
    penal code, 107; radicalized, 29;
    sophisticated culture, 32-3; Western
    perception/hostility, 3, 5, 13, 23, 31,
    34-5, 37, 39, 41, 48
Islambouli, Khalid al, 6, 71
Islamic Conference, March 1989, 61
Islamic Penal Code, 99
Islamic Salvation Front, Algeria (FIS), 4,
    6-7, 82-4
Islamic state, 97-8, 106; concept, 13, 75,
    78; duties, 77;
ideal, 69, 74
islamization, 18
Israel, 4, 14, 18, 89, 126; establishment
    of, 15; revisionist historians, 17; State
    of, 16, 28, 30

Jahilyyah, 72
Jamaat-e-Islami, 49, 61, 67, 71
Jamaat-e-Islami Hind, Central Advisory
    Council, 86
Jamal al-Din al-Afghani, 69
Jamiat Ulama-e-Hind, 61-2, 86
Jamiat Ulama-I-Islam Pakistan, 67
Jesus Christ, 48
Jewish Agency, 18, 80
Jewish people, fundamentalist, 65
jihad, 12, 23-4; concepts, 45-9, 51, 55-6,
    69, 74, 110; forms, 72; modern
    jihadists, 57-8; universal, 71
Jihad-e-Akbar, 118
John of Segovia, 36
Jordan, 4
Just World Trust, 58
justice: distributive, 100; social, 47, 114

Kalam Azad, Maulana Abul, 60, 108,
    115
Kashmir, 89
Kayani, M.R., 74
Keddie, Nikki R., 110

Participating Organizations

Both ENDS: A service and advocacy organization which collaborates with environment and indigenous organizations, both in the South and in the North, with the aim of helping to create and sustain a vigilant and effective environmental movement.
Damrak 28-30, 1012 LJ Amsterdam, The Netherlands
Tel: +31 20 623 0823   Fax: +31 20 620 8049
Email: info@bothends.org • Website: www.bothends.org

Catholic Institute for International Relations (CIIR): CIIR aims to contribute to the eradication of poverty through a programme that combines advocacy at national and international level with community-based development.
Unit 3 Canonbury Yard, 190a New North Road, London N1 7BJ, UK
Tel: +44 (0)20 7354 0883   Fax: +44 (0)20 7359 0017
Email: ciir@ciir.org • Website: www.ciir.org

Corner House: The Corner House is a UK-based research and solidarity group working on social and environmental justice issues in North and South.
PO Box 3137, Station Road, Sturminster Newton, Dorset DT10 1YJ, UK
Tel: +44 (0)1258 473795   Fax: +44 (0)1258 473748
Email: cornerhouse@gn.apc.org • Website: www.cornerhouse.icaap.org

Council on International and Public Affairs (CIPA): CIPA is a human rights research, education and advocacy group, with a particular focus on economic and social rights in the USA and elsewhere around the world. Emphasis in recent years has been given to resistance to corporate domination.
777 United Nations Plaza, Suite 3C, New York, NY 10017, USA.
Tel: +1 212 972 9877   Fax: +1 212 972 9878
Email: cipany@igc.org • Website: www.cipa-apex.org

Dag Hammarskjöld Foundation: The Dag Hammarskjöld Foundation, established 1962, organises seminars and workshops on social, economic and cultural issues facing developing countries with a particular focus on alternative and innovative solutions. Results are published in its journal *Development Dialogue*.
Övre Slottsgatan 2, 753 10 Uppsala, Sweden.
Tel: +46 18 102772   Fax: +46 18 122072
Email: secretariat@dhf.uu.se • web site: www.dhf.uu.se

Development GAP: The Development Group for Alternative Policies is a Non-Profit Development Resource Organization working with popular organizations in the South and their Northern partners in support of a development that is truly sustainable and that advances social justice.
927 15th Street, NW - 4th Floor, Washington, DC 20005 – USA
Tel: +1 202 898 1566   Fax: +1 202 898 1612
Email: dgap@igc.org • Website: www.developmentgap.org

Focus on the Global South: Focus is dedicated to regional and global policy analysis and advocacy work. It works to strengthen the capacity of organizations of the poor and marginalized people of the South and to better analyse and understand the impacts of the globalization process on their daily lives.
C/o CUSRI, Chulalongkorn University, Bangkok 10330, Thailand
Tel: +66 2 218 7363   Fax: +66 2 255 9976
Email: Admin@focusweb.org • Website: www.focusweb.org

Inter Pares: Inter Pares, a Canadian social justice organization, has been active since 1975 in building relationships with Third World development groups and providing support for community-based development programmes. Inter Pares is also involved in education and advocacy in Canada, promoting understanding about the causes, effects and solutions to poverty.
58 rue Arthur Street, Ottawa, Ontario, K1R 7B9 Canada
Tel: + 1 613 563 4801   Fax: + 1 613 594 4704

Public Interest Research Centre: PIRC is a research and campaigning group based in Delhi which seeks to serve the information needs of activists and organizations working on macro-economic issues concerning finance, trade and development.
142, Maitri Apartments, Plot No. 28, Patparganj, Delhi: 110092, India
Tel: + 91 11 2221081, 2432054   Fax: + 91 11 2224233
Email: kaval@nde.vsnl.net.in

Third World Network: TWN is an international network of groups and individuals involved in efforts to bring about a greater articulation of the needs and rights of peoples in the Third World; a fair distribution of the world's resources; and forms of development which are ecologically sustainable and fulfil human needs.
Its international secretariat is based in Penang, Malaysia.
228 Macalister Road, 10400 Penang, Malaysia
Tel: +60 4 226 6159   Fax: +60 4 226 4505
Email: twnet@po.jaring.my • Website: www.twnside.org.sg

Third World Network–Africa: TWN–Africa is engaged in research and advocacy on economic, environmental and gender issues. In relation to its current particular interest in globalization and Africa, its work focuses on trade and investment, the extractive sectors and gender and economic reform.
2 Ollenu Street, East Legon, P O Box AN19452, Accra-North, Ghana.
Tel: +233 21 511189/503669/500419   Fax: +233 21 511188
Email: twnafrica@ghana.com

World Development Movement (WDM): The World Development Movement campaigns to tackle the causes of poverty and injustice. It is a democratic membership movement that works with partners in the South to cancel unpayable debt and break the ties of IMF conditionality, for fairer trade and investment rules, and for strong international rules on multinationals.
25 Beehive Place, London SW9 7QR, UK
Tel: +44 (0)20 7737 6215   Fax: +44 (0)20 7274 8232
Email: wdm@wdm.org.uk • Website: www.wdm.org.uk

The GLOBAL ISSUES Series

Already available in English

Robert Ali Brac de la Perrière and Franck Seuret, *Brave New Seeds: The Threat of GM Crops to Farmers*

Walden Bello, *Deglobalization: New Ideas for Running the World Economy*

Oswaldo de Rivero, *The Myth of Development: The Non-viable Economies of the 21st Century*

Joyeeta Gupta, *Our Simmering Planet: What to do about Global Warming?*

Nicholas Guyatt, *Another American Century? The United States and the World after 2000*

Martin Khor, *Rethinking Globalization: Critical Issues and Policy Choices*

John Madeley, *Food for All: The Need for a New Agriculture*

John Madeley, *Hungry for Trade: How the Poor Pay for Free Trade*

A. G. Noorani, *Islam and Jihad: Prejudice versus Reality*

Riccardo Petrella, *The Water Manifesto: Arguments for a World Water Contract*

Vandana Shiva, *Protect or Plunder? Understanding Intellectual Property Rights*

Harry Shutt, *A New Democracy: Alternatives to a Bankrupt World Order*

David Sogge, *Give and Take: What's the Matter with Foreign Aid?*

In preparation

Peggy Antrobus, *The International Women's Movement: Issues and Strategies*

Amit Bhaduri and Deepak Nayyar, *Free Market Economics: The Intelligent Person's Guide to Liberalization*

Jonathan Bloch and Paul Todd, *Business as Usual? Intelligence Agencies and Secret Services in the New Century*

Julian Burger, *First Peoples: What Future?*

Graham Dunkley, *Free Trade: Myths, Realities and Alternatives*

Ha-Joon Chang and Ilene Grabel, *No Alternative? Myths and Realities about Economic Policy Choices*

Susan Hawley and Morris Szeftel, *Corruption: Privatization, Transnational Corporations and the Export of Bribery*

Roger Moody, *Digging the Dirt: The Modern World of Global Mining*

Peter Robbins, *The Commodities Disaster: What Can Be Done?*

Kavaljit Singh, *The Myth of Globalization: Ten Questions Everyone Asks*

Keith Suter, *Curbing Corporate Power: How Can We Control Transnational Corporations?*

Nedd Willard, *The War on Drugs: Is This the Solution?*

For full details of this list and Zed's other subject and general catalogues, please write to: The Marketing Department, Zed Books, 7 Cynthia Street, London N1 9JF, UK or email Sales@zedbooks.demon.co.uk

Visit our website at: http://www.zedbooks.demon.co.uk

THIS BOOK IS ALSO AVAILABLE IN THE FOLLOWING COUNTRIES:

EGYPT
MERIC (The Middle East
Readers' Information Center)
2 Bahgat Ali Street,
Tower D/Apt. 24
Zamalek, Cairo
Tel: 20 2 735 3818/736 3824
Fax: 20 2 736 9355

FIJI
University Book Centre
University of South Pacific,
Suva
Tel: 679 313 900
Fax: 679 303 265

GHANA
EPP Book Services
P O Box TF 490
Trade Fair
Accra
Tel: 233 21 773087
Fax: 233 21 779099

MAURITIUS
Editions Le Printemps
4 Club Road
Vacoas
Mauritius

MOZAMBIQUE
Sul Sensacoes
PO Box 2242,
Maputo
Tel: 258 1 421974
Fax: 258 1 423414

NAMIBIA
Book Den
PO Box 3469
Shop 4, Frans Indongo Gardens
Windhoek
Tel: 264 61 239976
Fax: 264 61 234248

NEPAL
Everest Media Services
GPO Box 5443, Dillibazar
Putalisadak Chowk
Kathmandu
Tel: 977 1 416026
Fax: 977 1 250176

PAKISTAN
Vanguard Books
45 The Mall
Lahore
Tel: 92 42 735 5079
Fax: 92 42 735 5197

PAPUA NEW GUINEA
Unisearch PNG Pty Ltd
Box 320, University
National Capital District
Tel: 675 326 0130
Fax: 675 326 0127

PHILIPPINES
IBON Foundation , Inc.
3rd Floor SCC Bldg.,
4427 Int. Old Sta. Mesa,
Manila, Philippines 1008
Tel.: (632) 713-2729 / 713-
2737
Fax: (632) 716-0108

RWANDA
Librairie Ikirezi
PO Box 443,
Kigali
Tel/Fax: 250 71314

SUDAN
The Nile Bookshop
New Extension Street 41
P O Box 8036
Khartoum
Tel: 249 11 463 749

TANZANIA
TEMA Publishing Co Ltd
PO Box 63115
Dar Es Salaam
Tel: 255 51 113608
Fax: 255 51 110472

UGANDA
Aristoc Booklex Ltd
PO Box 5130,
Kampala Road
Diamond Trust Building
Kampala
Tel/Fax: 256 41 254867

ZAMBIA
UNZA Press
PO Box 32379
Lusaka
Tel: 260 1 290409
Fax: 260 1 253952

ZIMBABWE
Weaver Press
PO Box A1922
Avondale
Harare
Tel: 263 4 308330
Fax: 263 4 339645